Spira

Signs for Healing

When a spiral is placed within a hand shape,
it is believed to be emitting energy.
It is a symbol of healing power,
constantly radiating from the cosmos
around us and helps us return
to the natural rhythm of the spiral
so we can fall back into healing harmony.

From southwestern USA. Also called
a Shaman's Hand or Healer's Hand

Linda Varsell Smith

Gyan Mudra

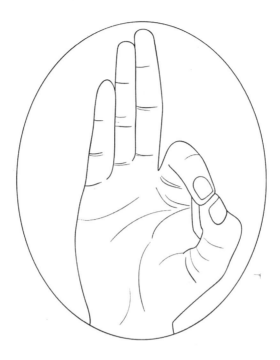

Mudra is a Sanskrit word meaning "gesture". With over 100 in existence, they are generally used in Hindu, Buddhist, and meditation practices. Usually done with the hands, each position symbolizes some form of energy flow affecting the body, mind, and/or spirit.

Gyan Mudra: The "gesture of consciousness" promotes expansion and knowledge, stimulating the root chakra, memory, and the brain, along with easing tension and stimulating the endocrine system. Holding this gesture while in meditation can also provide insights about your life or a particular issue depending on your intention.

The Position: join the tips of the index finger and thumb while holding the other three fingers straight. Apply the gesture to both hands, or combine with another mudra in the other hand.

Duration: While the general rule suggests holding a mudra for 15 minutes, some practices suggest 45 minutes while others suggest 2-3. Go with what feels right for you and gives you the most benefit.

- Maureen Frenk

Thanks to

Maureen Frank: The Mandala Lady
for preparing the manuscript for printing
and creating the wonderful artwork.

Drawings of Kip Smith by Susan Johnson

My poetry friends, critique groups.
intuitive consultants and family.

ISBN: 978-0-9888554-7-2

Rainbow Communications
471 NW Hemlock Ave.
Corvallis, OR 97330

varsell4@comcast.net

About Linda Varsell Smith

She is a teacher, poet and novelist
who lives in Corvallis, Oregon
in a mini-museum of her miniature collections of dollhouses,
angels, winged ones, Swedish folk art, seasonal decorations.
She taught creative writing, children's literature
and Write Your Life Story at Linn-Benton Community College.
She gives poetry workshops and readings,
sponsors youth writing contests, judges all ages of poetry.
Linda was an editor at Calyx Books for 32 years
and LBCC's The Eloquent Umbrella magazine instructor.
Former president of the Oregon Poetry Association,
current president Portland PEN Women,
she belongs to several writing groups,
Writing the Wrongs to Rights Huddle,
plays competitive and cooperative Scrabble.
She's a great fan of dance, gymnastics, plays and art.

Table of Contents

Chi

Spirit

Cycles

Spirals

Dreams

Rituals

Cosmos

Circles

Chi

Circulating life energy that in Chinese philosophy
is thought to be inherent in all things.
In traditional Chinese Medicine the balance
of positive and negative forms in the body
is believed to be essential to good health.
In Taoism chi means air or breath
and is the energy flow or life force
prevalent in all things.
Chi flows through the body in body pathways
known as meridians (energy pathways)
and chakras (energy centers).
Chi maintains health and wellness,
mentally, physically, emotionally and spiritually.

Butterflies

This lovely June solstice afternoon,
I went into the backyard to breathe some chi,
trying to increase my energy. To fly.

I sat on the crusty, mossy sidewalk wall
chunked together overlooking our clover
and buttercup spotted lawn.

Two aborted apples underneath its branch,
mold on the doors of the beige storage shed.
Grayish plastic rubbish bin. Ladder–sideways.

Flowers past bloom. Cherries undetectable.
Fencing keeps out most deer, a few dogs.
Cats probably hidden in the bushes.

Two stellar jays flit to a hazelnut limb.
Shadows overlay the lush lawn.
Two wind chimes ring in the breeze.

I sat on the wall inhaling Gaia's chi
and exhaling celestial energy.
My feet still encased in black SAS shoes.

I chose shade since when I did
meditate outside regularly-- a while ago--
I developed skin cancer on my nose.

Two healers told me to connect
with the earth and sky for my health and poems.
I decided to try again.

An intuitive saw me as a butterfly frantically flapping
my wings, yet staying in place like a hummingbird.
I needed to breathe deeply for momentum to fly.

I'm huffing and puffing hot air
when a solitary yellow butterfly fluttered by.
I smiled at my signal. I'm flying.

Absorbing Gaia's Chi

I go to the backyard under cloudless blue sky
to soak in Gaia's chi, give meditation a try
beneath pear, peach, apple, hazelnut canopy.

I situate my waiting, red canvas camp chair
to strategically place it with some care
in shade, facing east to relax and be aware.

The clover-buttercup dotted grass wriggles freely.
Bugs flit by, but don't bother me.
Two white butterflies wing-it erratically.

One blue bird flies east, a black bird flies west.
No birds appeared to visit or nest.
No creatures interfere with my rest.

The apple tree is taller than our house and sways.
Top bobbled with unripe, un-fallen fruit–it stays,
but I could get bopped if windfall apple preys.

A new bird feeder and wooden wind-chimes--
belated Mother's and Father's Day gifts primes
new tinkling sounds and happy bird times.

Shadows shiver in balmy breeze,
wind-dancing amid the leaf-shaking trees.
I practice a deep belly-breath wheeze.

I'm to open my root chakra, aid healing,
but find my senses stirred and reeling.
Will the sun burn my face to peeling?

Nature is beautiful, dangerous, alluring--
but my safe backyard is reassuring
my restful mini-staycation is re-occurring.

The Hand Mower

When the sun shines, it shines for everyone. Ziggy Marley

Sitting in the backyard sipping celestial and terrestrial chi,
I watch my husband morning-mow the scraggly lawn.
This afternoon's temperature should reach 100.

He uses a reel mower because it is good exercise,
produces no pollution, is less noisy, handles well.
He rotates mowing four directions and two diagonals.

His push mower's seven blades cut like scissors.
He gave away his weed-whacker type mower
for a cleaner cut and lets clippings supply nitrogen.

He pulls weeds to toss into a white bucket.
Wind-broken twigs join a compost bin.
Clover and buttercup tops lopped off.

He talks about setting up hoses, further weeding.
The front yard gets closer attention first—
yesterday's priority in his yard work tasks.

The cut grass blades flatten. Too uniform
butch cut for me–I prefer a longer, layered look.
I enjoy pop spots of color, not monotonous green.

He says the peaches are not producing.
The cherries are mostly lost to borers.
Well, we usually lose them to hungry birds.

He pushes hard, his hand mower over uneven terrain--
a small-lawn-senior-Shiva- manifesting
destruction before creation under sweating sun.

Contrails

A north/south contrail wafts eastward
marking a cloudless sky
with a diffusing, morphing scar.

The contrail widens, fringes
from the east side, bubbles west
striates, releases wispy ribs.

To the west a small plane
merely scratches sky.
Contrail dissolves quickly.

To the east a larger contrail
thrusts north, gushes another
plume. Will the contrails merge?

These artificial clouds criss-cross,
mar other layers of clouds,
intersect into endless patterns.

Condensed water vapor, ice crystals
adding to acid rain dripping down
on the terrestrials below.

Gazing at the transforming clouds
holds endless fascination,
when un-sliced by contrails.

Backyard News

Clear sky-- no clouds or contrails
except to the east a UFO cloud
dispersing into air.

Shadows wind-dance under trees
on the golf-course lawn with a few
defiant stalks un-bowed, un-clipped.

When the children were young,
tin can golf holes dug in the grass
provided many mini-golf games.

Now the holes are filled with dirt.
Some apple, cherry, hazelnut branches
have died to crusty brown.

Organic fruit and nuts battle
borers, worms, scaly blemishes.
One peach. Diminished harvest.

Across the yard, blue jays and LBJs
chatter, bounce branches, compete
with wind-chimes' knell.

Trunks and limbs host moss, blotches,
roughened bark. Apple branches bend
like sway-backs. Limbs not too perky.

My debris-dusted camp chair faces north
under overhang-shade. Leaf-lacing view above.
I forgot my distant glasses, so all is blurry.

Conjuring Crop Circles

Contemplating crop circles, I walk
to my camp chair for a daily dose of chi
under a gauzy blue summer sky.

What would it be like to have
an up-close and personal crop circle
imprinted in my own back yard?

Apparently various humanoid E.T. species
create increasingly complex crop circles,
beginning with one circle and expanding.

Crop circles form flowers of life, Fibonacci
sequence, pi and vesica pisces patterns,
as well as Metatron's cube, sacred geometry.

The design spirals outward. Chakras spin,
yang and yin unite and expand as one,
in the holistic language of light,

suggesting one consciousness
experienced in diverse fragments,
in self-organizing systems like torus.

I do not have tall grain stalks
for energy to heat and twist
into 3D cosmic symbols.

I have scruffy grass- ground whiskers.
Perhaps E.T.s could brand a burn?
Leave black ash instead of bending blades?

Crop circles could contain the truth
of the universe in light-encoded symbols
from multi-dimensional technology.

Created by electro-magnetic energy in minutes
they convey symbolic blocks of coded information
from E.T. light beings in light language.

A black and white cat stares away birds,
then hides in the bushes for a hunter's blind
or to privately poop. E.T.'s more overt?

Authentic crop circles are precise perfection,
not messy like the fake ones made by man. Maybe
a lawn tattoo could appear instantaneously?

The only unnatural design in the lawn
is a green garden hose slithering
through the closely cropped grass.

Only a scattering of crimped leaves,
yard shadows, tree trunks pattern the lawn,
as I conjure crop circles at my feet.

I read when we need to understand
the symbols implanted at the subconscious level
then we will intuit the light-encoded information.

We are in a transition time. Some people
feel increased harmonic vibrations
or become telepathic in a crop circle.

Some propose our pineal glands and hearts
will expand to create with dimensions
of intelligence and to understand crop circles.

Until then I can imagine my own crop circles,
recall my favorite designs. Mine, maybe not
math-based, but free-form splashes of color.

Garden-Gazer

Technically our backyard is not a garden.
It is a multiple-use area – some garden,
berry patch, mini-orchard, and butchered lawn.

Especially in good weather I try
to commune with cultivated nature,
sitting in a camp chair, absorbing Gaia's chi.

Today I saw a rare hummingbird among
the black and blue bruise of birds
checking out the joint un-harassed.

I wonder what my yard would say to me?
The clover and buttercups might
appreciate my not considering them a weed?

The bushes wave thanks for
letting them fade without plucking,
not chasing fertilizing cats and dogs?

The cherries, apples, hazelnuts, peach
allowed to ripen and windfall without
my interference, expand in the sun?

Blueberries and strawberries un-nuzzled
by noses of deer, since side fences
protect all our organic produce.

I admire the texture on tree trucks,
the splotches of gray, the fuzzy moss,
the crustiness of their bark,

the craggy, stacked, sidewalk wall
blemished by growths, stalks stringing out,
doing back-breaking work holding back earth.

The tightly cropped lawn stretches again,
knowing I advocate for crab grass, dandelions,
buttercups and clover–diversity?

Leaves waver in the wind, fall and crunch beige.
I did not break the dangling spider thread.
Jangling wind-chimes clink a background rhythm.

The backyard in gusty chorus might sing:
"Thanks for your benign neglect, gratefully
your hands-off approach, lets us all be free."

9

Cacophonies

Midday was not the best time today
to sit in the sun to catch a ray.
A very noisy place, I would say.

First, the fenced-in back neighbor
let loose an intermittent motor roar.
Sawing down a tree? What for?

Then another mower's mutter,
started to spit and sputter,
with choice words, he chose to utter.

Then ever present in the background
is the murmur of distant traffic sound
and a train's whistle southbound.

A rattling truck rumbled by
adding loud music. I try
to tune out with a sigh.

The bird's are a chatty bunch
as they stop by for lunch,
or take a break is my hunch.

The wind-chimes ding-a-ling,
with the leaves gentle rustling.
At least my mobile phone didn't ring.

So much for quiet, tranquil meditating.
Such unnatural and natural noise is irritating,
but Scrabble players' laughs I'm anticipating.

Be Happy

It might seem crazy what I'm about to say.
Sunshine's she's here, you can take a break.
Pharrel Williams "Happy"

Sunday, July 2nd of July 4th weekend
I went into the backyard to soak in some sun
with the intention of focusing on happy thoughts.

I hummed Pharrel Williams' "Happy" song.
I'm welcomed by soothing, soughing winds
summer-warmth and clear skies.

The green hose snakes to the garden.
Unheard, my husband mows the front yard.
The jingle of wind-chimes sparks spritely thoughts.

This mid-morning many people are in church,
others communing with nature, celebrating
with barbecues, family picnics and fireworks.

Clap along if you know what happiness is to you.

Beforehand, I clipped newspaper articles to provoke poems,
patriotic symbols to illustrate my weekly Smith Family
Chronicle, recording family events since 1963.

My latest book will be mailed across country
and overseas after the holiday. I've already
given local family and friends copies.

Unexpectedly and delightfully early,
my Stressless blue chair arrived from Norway
adding significantly to my seated pleasure.

The last few days have been muse-full
and mostly good news for me personally
and for several loved ones.

Here come bad news, talking this and that.

But today Trump whined MSNBC was biased.
Fox News kisses his ass, why not other networks kick it?
I vowed to stay on happy track and not watch news today.

Can't nuthing bring me down

This Fourth of July promises some happy events--
a baseball game with fireworks, grandson's visit,
local parade, out of town fireworks display.

When I widen my scope world-wide,
or limit contemplation to our American Dream,
the pursuit of happiness feels compromised.

I try to shift my concentration
from this camp chair to my new blue chair,
from environmental destruction, to our well-tended yard.

Tears begin spilling down my cheeks.
I do not know if they are tears of sadness
or tears of joy. Maybe both.

Clap along if you feel like that's what you want to do.

I'll Trust My Ding

Sipping unsweetened green tea,
        relaxing in my red camp chair,
I watch our grandson mow the backyard
        with a reel push mower.

The lawn is littered with windfall apples,
        tan leaves from dead limbs.
He whops the tops of white clover,
        pops them like popcorn.

When he is done, he sits in a blue chair
        beside me and takes out his Android.
He selects clash, bash, trash music
        from Foo Fighters, Nirvana, Butthole Surfers.

And a few other bands, I fortunately could not hear
        the lyrics most of the time. Finally
I had to ding the dang concert and negativity.
        I went inside to the ding-dong of wind chimes.

Louise Hay says we all have an "inner Ding"
        an "inner knowing" which serves to guide us.
Well, that music sent my ding ringing loud and clear.
        I just could not take in any more of the noise.

I'll trust my ding to tune out offensive music.
        My poor chakras probably spun like dervishes.
My angels and guides probably were not grooving.
        My feet were not dancing, left my heart pounding.

Keeping Cool

Today it is six before I mosey to the backyard,
green peach tea in hand to catch some of Gaia's chi.

It was hot today, so I dawdled until
ocean breezes moved inland, cooled early evening.

I am in a short-sleeved, red tee-shirt and blue shorts.
Just white socks on my feet. Cast off shoes hours ago.

Shadows stretch east across the lawn,
a cloudless, contrail-less sky does not filter sun.

Tan leaves drop from dead branches.
Clover recover from mower-lopped heads.

I have revived this ritual of relaxing and contemplating
in a camp chair. A fair-weather meditator and observer.

It is supposed to ground me. Connect me to the earth.
Enhance my root chakra energy. Today I am here later.

This morning I edited three sections of *Mirabilia*. Mid-day
went to the art center and gift shops to find a gift rooster.

This afternoon I napped and wrote two poems
about hypervelocity stars and spiritual education.

I will not get hot-headed about world affairs, but
will watch a documentary on Amelia Earhart mystery.

First I need to heat up a piece of chicken
to go with a pre-mixed, scraggly salad.

I hobble on patio pebbles gouging soles,
drag sock-dirt inside to sweep away.

The Summer Shift

On July 10th I can see summer changes.
Back lawn patches tan in the sun, will revive
in autumn rains-- until then, un-watered.

The cherry tree discards so many leaves,
they should be gone by fall in its slow dying.
One stalk treelet defiantly resists mowing.

Two white butterflies and a lone, low plane
fly west. Green hose tangles like veggie spaghetti.
Apples bauble on branches.

Three buttercups join the clover.
Few wind chimes or bird-chirps.
I relax in shade for a few minutes.

Inside the house I changed 4th of July decorations
for a sunflower print tablecloth, fake sunflower
bouquet surrounded by dolls in sunflower fabric.

A grandson starts a new job today.
A granddaughter prepares to move.
My husband recovers from a burst eardrum.

Allergies provoke sneezes everywhere.
Getting monthly B-12 shot at clinic this morning,
strangers exchange prayers for their maladies.

Probably few long-sleeved days for awhile.
Air-conditioning will remain in service.
My daily commitments and rituals–routine.

The newspapers blare riots in Germany
over G-20 Summit where Trump chums
with Putin and alienates about everyone else.

In DC, gratefully, health care debate is at standstill.
I recall yesterday–two Portland poetry readings
of six poets, prime ribs with my first publisher.

What a shift in locality, sounds in a day!
Such different experiences of summer.
I appreciate a tranquil respite–a nap.

Writing Reverie

It was late afternoon before I went
into the backyard for my daily dose of Gaia chi.
Lawn shadows sprawled east in sea breeze.

After two afternoon visits with writerly friends,
I lugged a lukewarm, fast food feast
with green peach tea and plopped in the chair.

The first visit I went to my cosmic, poet friend's.
The second visit a more grounded poet came to me.
I had just zipped through the drive-through.

So by the time I plunked the bag on an adjoining
chair and ice-melted tea in chair pocket,
the food was not in peak condition.

Between the slats in the back fence
I could see my sneezing neighbor
spraying or watering near the fence.

I reflected on my visits and information
I gleaned from their endeavors, then recalled
my exercise class asking about my writing process.

It was difficult to explain what I do not fully
understand. I am curious about something,
mull and muse, then I'm guided or channeled.

I wake in the night to write down lines.
I jot notes on paper at hand–anywhere.
Some energy tells me to pay attention.

I research my interests and the form
flows to the content of the poem. I compose
on the computer directly or on paper.

The bag is filled with litter, tea half-gone.
My neighbor appears to be spraying.
My husband is back from a bike ride.

Time to go inside, still full of questions. Word-play
and creative process allows my existence to dance
with the cosmos. My soul-sliver records insights I find.

Writing Reverie #2

It is near noon as I bumble into the backyard carrying
a bag with plain hot dog and sauce-less chicken nuggets,
on special, and glass of cran-pomegranate juice.

Tucked under the roof shadow, I begin munching
and sipping, contemplating what I did not say
about my writing process to my T/Th exercise class.

The stellar jays flit branch to branch, hop on grass
poking and pecking, flush competitors from their lunch.
Back-blushed jay pays no attention to me and strolls nearby.

All this flutter distracts me, however from my intention.
As we eat in front of each other, they ignore me.
I have no tidbits to share. They find their own fast food.

Inside at the computer I ruminate on my writing process.
I can't remember a time without poetry-- spoke in rhyme
at 3, dictated rhymed quatrains at 6 and illustrated them.

I have studied poetry before college, in college, after
college, taught poetry to all ages as well as college,
attended and taught at many conferences and workshops.

I read poetry from around the world with Calyx Press,
coordinated a college arts journal, sent out some poems
and collected them into chapbooks and books.

I love to word-play, dance words down the line,
discover new forms, invent some, puzzle what approach
is best for each form and listen to my muse.

I like to explore ideas, expose mysteries, ask reader
to look at life from their own perspective and keep learning.
I do not want to convert anyone to anything. I'll open choices.

My M/W/F exercise class have also commented on my poems.
A born-again Christian said she was praying for me.
Today another reader brought me a book of Emily Dickinson.

I am on the Poet's Journey– not expecting to be a hero/ine.
I ponder, wonder and do not expect I'll ever have all the answers.
I just love words, combining their sounds and meanings into dance.

I am a word-junkie. When it's too hot or I'm too lazy
to cook, I also eat junk food. Heaven is dark chocolate
or a digested poem as dessert.

Slurry

Mid-day I slogged to the backyard
for my ritual dosing of Gaia and cosmic chi.
It was overcast, so no shadows laced the lawn.

After exercise class and acupuncture
I was too drained to grocery shop.
My husband helped me carry my fast food lunch.

He even brought me a cardboard box
to place my food upon as I drooped
into the sagging chair.

After exercise class chit-chatting,
Sarah brought boy brownies with nuts
(pecans) and girl brownies without bits.

At acupuncture she supposedly needled
energy flow, removed toxins, removed
energy and mucous blockages.

Still my energy felt slurry, blood moving thickly,
muscles aching—a limp dishrag as I wobbled
into the backyard and munched lunch.

The birds must be pick-nicking elsewhere.
Perhaps the mower motor of our diagonal neighbor
annoyed them as well, they dine somewhere more tranquil.

Weak wind does not play with wind-chimes.
Only sound is the non-stop moan-groan
of the revving mower, hammering my head.

Idea-interference for my sleepy brain.
When time's up—I go inside muting the motor.
After a nap, cooperative Scrabble should revive me.

This is just one of those very-slow, low energy days
which require a higher dosage of dark chocolate--
might not really help, but you think it does.

Seeing Things Differently
Theme for Da Vinci Days July 14-16 2017
Corvallis, Oregon, Benton County Fairgrounds

Midday sitting in my backyard in a Da Vinci Days tee shirt,
I reflect on yesterday's celebration of Science, Technology,
Art, Music and Food, including activities for all ages.

In honor of Leonardo, the art and science genius,
Da Vinci Days is making a comeback with volunteers
and sponsors on a lesser scale than former glory.

The highlight for me is the Grand Kinetic Challenge
where imaginative human-powered, engineering vehicles
pedal over land, river race, sand dune climb and mud bog slog.

Sixteen entries came to compete with design, speed,
jokes, bribes, trading cards, original songs for prizes
in many categories: artistry, pageantry and engineering.

Our children and grandchildren loved the parade and feats.
This year we went child-less and skipped sand dune
and mud bog, but enjoyed the creativity of the teams.

I picked up cards from Spacely Sprockets and A Cockwork
Orange, a small flag from Ladybugs. Other crews had names
like Area 52, Team Funguy, Soul Train in "Triathlon of the Art World."

The art building featured an ekphrasis exhibit of art and poetry
based on Da Vinci, arts and crafts. Under tents outside--
the science exhibits: innovations from HP, 3D printing items.

Oregon State and Linn-Benton Community college
had free glasses and information on upcoming solar eclipse.
I bought two eclipse tee-shirts to support their sponsors.

A new bus to train connection will begin-- shiny new.
Governmental services telling what they do.
Delicious food booths to sip and chew.

I manage to drop and bend bow to my glasses, get
sun screen in my eye, hold weeping in handkerchief,
but enjoy—drops a delicious French dip sandwich.

I heard the silly songs of the Kinetic sculpture teams,
under the shade of a tent. As we left Taiwanese singers
and dancers performed similarly to Native Americans.

I came home with pens, pamphlets, eclipse glasses,
HP gave blue paper flower embedded with seeds
with instructions how to plant it. Paper recycles in soil.

We had attended the lecture by Dr. Tim Weber of HP
on "3D Printing and the Coming Revolution." He calls
this the fourth industrial revolution which will be local.

No longer ship raw materials to China with finished
products shipped back. Stuff will be built in your town.
Robot trucks roam roadways. Jobs lost. Some left behind.

The technical talk left some of the audience puzzled.
He answered questions on recycling, sustainability,
applications, the impacts of accelerated innovation.

My mind buzzes with the different ways of seeing,
the imagination, innovation, the art, science whizzing
around at a dizzying pace. It's wonderfully outside the box.

I'm sitting in upgraded backyard lawn furniture—
a black metal, open weave armed chair and a blue metal,
hourglass-shaped, rods cinched at middle, round table.

It replaces the camp chair and adds a place to plunk
food or drink as I meditate. A black and blue bruise
on the lawn where I muse, see things differently.

HONEY and the Chakra Check

The true hero quests within. There is no dragon to slay. There is no war to win. There is no mountain to climb. There is only the landscape of what is within, which is you in the Universe. Which is you as one of the now in the Now. Which is also you, as an earth being, with an earth heart, surrounding and infinitely connecting to all living beings. This is the hero's quest for no chalice, no sword, no banner. The hero's quest in this time is for connection, it is for compassion, it is for love. This is the task of the world you are in now.
Sara Wiseman from The 33 Lessons

Early afternoon under a cloudless sky in the backyard,
I sit and ponder what energy signature is trying to get
my attention and connect. Why? I look for omens.

A windfall apple plops in front of me. A clump of fuzz
from a dead branch is like a gigantic clover
with real white clover clustered around.

A white butterfly, a bug, small bird flit by.
A black cat with white nose strolls through
the yard into our neighbor's.

An orange round basket full of gladiola blades
left on the wall. My husband harvested blueberries
and has the hose snake to water strawberries.

Birds have a gab fest. Wind-chimes tinkle
in the gentle breeze. The mobile phone is silent.
I am not sensing any clues from this Gaia chi quest.

At the last cooperative Scrabble game, the first
five tiles I turned over spelled HONEY, the name
everyone called my mother. What is the urgency?

We've spelled her name in several games, but not
as the starting word, the first five of nine tiles.
We welcome her presence and play the game.

Maybe it was to warn me of my chakra test.
My massage therapist found a disturbing large
black cord in my heart chakra which is usually clear.

We called on my angels and guides to pull it out
like we did with an orange chakra cord before.
I try to protect myself from energetic hitch-hikers.

Then when I woke in the night, my digital clock
displayed the angel number 444. Is that my signal
the issue has been resolved by my higher self?

At times the contact with other energy signatures
remains unclear until a shaman or intuitive
can connect with the cosmos and deliver the message.

How am I to interpret HONEY and the Chakra check results?
Is 444 the answer or a call for me to look deeper within?
All is energy and consciousness. Where do I look?

In Appreciation of the Inca

On "Time Scanners", scientists used
laser scans and ground penetrating radar
to create point clouds of data to understand
the mysteries of Machu Picchu in Peru.

Magnificent sky-city amid sacred mountains,
Inca had advanced engineering not possible today:
the water ditches, bonded masonry, earthquake proof
perfect stone buildings, observatories, temples, terraced crops.

Ingenious Inca protected their emperor and court,
created sites for their rituals, provided elements
possible for a civilization to thrive-- before it was gobbled
in jungle, then re-discovered in 1920s.

I stare at the backyard sidewalk chunks, "ruble wall"
we actually built without mortar like the Inca.
It is a remnant from our self-sustainable period.
This wall holds back a terrace for gardening.

We had fruit trees and berries, so the terrace
raised vegetables. Over the years, grass was allowed
to return to more of a putting green. Not much
of a nourishing garden left now–just the berries.

In our aqua-culture phase, my husband,
a mechanical engineer turned anthropologist,
extended the wall into a pond, tried to seal
with plastic and siphon rain from the roof.

The water went under ground up into the pond.
A drain released excess rainwater. Again like the Inca
we were training water flow, as we started raising fish.
We had a pair of tilapia–which died from overfeeding.

Someone gave us a Willamette carp which he froze
and it revived in the pond, until scarfed by a heron we think.
Finally a thriving school of goldfish, until a leak lowered
the water level and the goldfish were easy picking.

Our neighbors had young children–ours were older.
He dismantled the pond fearing drowning. The fish
were gone, pond disheveled. The sidewalk chunks
recycled into sides to form a compost area–which works.

My husband required back surgery lifting
and placing the sidewalk chunks into walls
for the terrace and pond. He still mows with
a reel mower which is more environmentally friendly.

The main yard is lawn dotted by fruit trees,
a place for games. Cherry tree dying,
veggies abandoned like Machu Picchu.
Our experiments failed, but we had good intentions.

Without the wheel, written language, steep slopes,
heavy boulders, Inca carved a mountain marvel.
I perform my chi rituals facing our lower cobbled wall,
water in a glass in camp chair's arm holder.

But I can visualize Machu Picchu, study
astronomy like the Inca, even though we ditched
the wheel barrow, wall building, terrace production.
I admire the Inca who were in harmony with nature.

Dancing Diversely

A gentle breeze choreographs leaves
and the flow of the shadows below
to the accompaniment of wind-chimes.

An ant round dances on the blushing skin
of a windfall apple, as nearby a spider strand
swings and twirls a curled leaf.

A white butterfly solos, fluttering
across the lawn, then exits on cue.
I am the silent audience.

I am reflecting on dancers- the ones
competing on So You Think You Can Dance
and tonight on World of Dance.

Daily, I ungracefully dress, trying
to get legs into pants and feet
into socks and shoes. Not dancerly.

I vicariously dance in memories
and watch dancers on stage and screen,
enjoying their lightening moves.

Less flexible in limbs, I try
to word-dance down the line--
a line dancer or maybe a chorus line?

Adaptable Chairs

My new, black, backyard chair
feels like sitting on a throne
as I survey my shady queendom.

I adjust the chair--full frontal
on even ground so I don't twist
positions as I look side to side.

In front of me is a two-foot, tree-let--
one leaf shining dew or goo, sparkling
like the diamond ring on my finger.

Inside we have been buying new chairs
to adapt to mostly my changing capacities.
I'm too slow for musical chairs.

At my computer cove, I've upgraded
to a comfortable chair with arms
which swivels on a plastic mat.

In the kitchen, the wooden, clunky, arm chair
from my father's office, chewing the cork
floor was replaced by a mobile chair on wheels.

I can glide to get silverware, zip to fridge,
hold the sturdy wooden back to get tableware before
eating and reading papers at the Hoosier cabinet.

In the TV room a rocker masticated the floor
and was unstable to rise from. My Norwegian
stressless chair caresses you in comfort.

Our grandson loves the rocker in his home now.
When he visits, he enjoys my new blue charmer
which hugs and supports us all.

In my bedroom I have an IKEA white plastic chair--
a dressing chair, since I need to climb 33 inches up
two steps to double captain's bed with 12 drawers to sit.

My husband decided to have four crusty, badly finished
dining room chairs, tossed from my father's job, refurbished.
They actually have great grain and a little shine.

They are additional seating for guests, writing groups
and our Huddle–Writing the Wrongs. The chairs
maybe change positions, but the sitters-- pretty staunch.

There are two rocking chairs for the rockers in the living room
as well. We offer seating options. Pillows on a metal bench
before a non-functional wood stove. A woven-seat Shaker chair.

My husband already made wooden cradles under couches
to raise them for elderly people to plop gracefully and easily.
They are easier to clean under as well.

He swaps his office chair according to his latest
theory which chair works best at a certain time.
We shift our discards until a perfect fit.

Tall toilets with hand rails, antique chairs from parents,
Hitchcock stenciled chairs around table in our gathering
room for family, friends, writers and Scrabblers.

Most chairs are made of wood, many with us
over 50 years. The new chairs, adapting
to our aging needs cushion us.

Intrusions

A white fluff floated by, probably
a dandelion from neighbor's yard
which has an abundant crop.

The silent soloists: rose, gladiola,
the yellow butterfly are joined
by a gray squirrel with white belly.

The squirrel scampered up
the apple tree and climbed down
with chosen apple from among hundreds.

He chomped away near the wall.
When satisfied, he zig-zagged down to lawn
to the top of wall several times–sniffing.

He clambered up the green hose,
dodged bullying birds trying to unnerve him,
snuffled across the lawn for apples.

When squirrel was just a few feet from me,
my husband slammed the door to come
out to tell me he was leaving to exercise.

The startled squirrel darted to the less
fruitful apple tree and nuzzled into a notch,
nose peering out one side, tail poking out other.

There he remained, I felt I'd treed him.
He seemed to have trusted me before
the door slam. Now he appeared jittery.

Around him the birds twittered unafraid,
tweeting puzzling tweets like Trump.
The wind chimes rang for squirrel's perch.

Some aggressive birds would flash- fly-by
to intimidate the squirrel, as if this were their turf.
Birds browse with ease lawn or canopy.

Two white, more dense, puffs drifted
before me. Wonder what weed they were?
The yard traffic was heavy today.

In my recent return to backyard chi dosing,
I had not seen a squirrel, nor nutria, raccoon
nor deer, only pets. Where are they intruding?

But then aren't I intruding into their space?
I am a temporary tenant of this land,
just like they are, sharing Gaia's chi.

Indigenous peoples have the right idea, protect
the planet for all creatures. Like our yard sign says:
Wherever you come from, you are welcome here.

What the Rose Said to the Glad

Not sure how much Gaia and cosmic chi
I'm ingesting through feet or head in the roof shadow
sitting on metal chair, SAS shoes on hard clay.

The clay, cracked crust hosting browning grass,
could leak chi through openings, plus worm and ant
dwellers. Ants follow blunt, bent blade routes.

The remaining red rose, crowded in shade
of bush shrouds, near the fence is the sole survivor
of its family branch, as is the solo gladiola.

The solitary orange gladiola on a flat patch
can snatch sun. Little shade
from the deteriorating cherry tree nearby.

Perhaps they chat about the fate
of the dying cherry neighbor. Perhaps
they overheard rumors of the chop down.

Surely they have noticed the decline
of the bird cherry-snackers
of the few cherries to ripen.

Perhaps the flowers are lonely.
No floral companions. No cherry chums.
What about apples or hazelnuts?

The cutting off of the dead hazelnut branch
probably was a omen of cherry tree's fate
and a reminder of their limited time left.

If everything has energy and consciousness,
humanity has no idea what other species experience,
let alone ourselves–let alone in the cosmos.

What the rose said to the gladiola—
I have no idea. No concept of their lives.
How does any being face death?

Bearing Witness

We know what to do: seek justice, love, mercy, walk humbly, treat every person as if she were yourself. These are not complicated instructions. It's much harder to decipher the instructions for putting together a tricycle than it is to understand these. Nancy Mairs

Late morning I adjust my backyard chair
on uneven ground to seek cover
from the roof shadow.

Clouds encroach from the west,
but the skies are clear overhead.
Ants climb grass blades from hard clay earth.

The dead hazelnut branch is gone,
droplets of lichen and moss remain
on the thirsty, dying lawn.

A red rose lingers alone beside the fence.
Nearby a solo orange gladiola partners color.
Plastic garden buckets stacked and stashed away.

I recall the persist and resist witness of our Huddle.
Eye-ball rolling Trump's twitter, bumbling incompetents,
disastrous acts and attacks on citizens and environment.

We are seven grandmothers trying to protect
our children's and grandchildren's future.
We are weary of petitions, marches, meetings.

We are tired of endless e-mails and causes
all wanting a donation. Good intentions, but
why can't our government just do their job?

We have an agenda, reports on different areas
like gerrymandering, health care, Indivisible
actions, upcoming town hall meetings etc. etc.

One woman wrote an essay on what she plans to do,
read, attend to, to avoid becoming overwhelmed
and too depressed to persist and resist.

She says she is frightened and angry and despondent.
She has lost heart and perspective; energy and religion.
She loses sleep; hope, joy and focus.

Each day she assesses what she must do,
what does she want to do. Is there anything to celebrate?
What she is grateful for? We are all exhausted.

Another member questions how we can keep going.
How do we maintain momentum? We have family
responsibilities and other commitments. Granny grit?

Johanna Macy suggests spinning a strand in the web of life.
Join with other strands in this world-wide web. Keep
informed, share concerns, and include them in your actions.

We can consider spinning our parts of the web
and where we can contribute. Wherever you meditate,
find where you can take action for a better world.

Along with other Huddles, we can remain open-minded,
open-hearted, work for the benefit of all. However, we are
united in our revulsion of tweety-Trump and company.

So as I finish my Gaia sun session,
I will go inside and work on a plan to oppose,
what I can't bear witnessing.

Energetic Reflections

At 2:00 I went into the backyard to peruse,
after the clouds allowed sun and warmth
to penetrate with some energizing vibes.

Lichen-flakes, moss-puffs, pine cones, leaves,
windfall apples joined clover and buttercups
to color and texture the browning, butch-cut lawn.

The metal table reflected white cloud patterns--
a round blue patch of sky. Ants attracted
to an empty table explored. One found my arm.

A bug buzzed my head, perhaps smelling
lunch lamb on my lips. Wind-chimes sluggishly knelled.
A solitary bird pecked near strawberries.

Green moss blanches on branches
as tanned leaves leave the limb. Next year
our red cherries could follow the downturn.

I was witnessing a mixed bag of activities.
Ahead I faced a fun, cooperative Scrabble game
then the urgency of our Huddle's serious issues.

I hobble inside, not overly energized
for either activity. I am sure I'll revive
my passions for both events.

How much Gaia's chi and cosmic rays
did I absorb? Shoes and skull too thick?
I hope to re-energize. Ah, dark chocolate.

The Universe Doesn't Do Random

Remember the Universe doesn't do random. If something shows up, it is a gift–a sign for you to ponder. Sara Wiseman

The backyard is staging the daily drama.
Stage left-a dangling apple on droopy branchlet,
catches sunlight-patch from the shade.

Mid-stage windfall apples constellate
into a new pattern. The hose position
has wriggled, loopy, shifted left.

Stage right–as if on cue, blue birds flew
to the blueberry bush to flesh out a feast.
Quarts-full had been picked.

In the background various types of birdcalls,
from mourning dove to stellar jay squawks
in syncopated rhythms with wind chimes.

It is before the lunch crowd. Most of the crew
is still and silent. An ant crawls near my sox-feet.
I am not the director in my nightgown.

Is this happening as part of a cosmic computer
program? Is this random or not? Signs to ponder?
Whatever life's placement, it is a gift.

A Mourning Dove Coos

As I walk into the backyard
a windfall apple plops to the ground.
          A mourning dove coos.

An apple constellation is askew
Pleiades or lopsided Big Dipper.
          A mourning dove coos.

My neighbor motor-mows his lawn
grating nerves, peace and quiet.
          A mourning dove coos.

Declared dead cherry tree drops tan leaves
too early to fall, awaits its chop down.
          A mourning dove coos.

When do the apples die? When stem
releases? Their silver cord?
Does the cherry tree die when sawn?

People are said to die when the silver cord
is severed. No matter where you travel
awake or asleep- it's life's umbilical cord?

As the wind-chimes knell, as the apples
fall various distances from their tree,
          a mourning dove coos.

Train of Thought

The orange gladiolas welcomed
some late-bloomers– a mini-splash
of sunrise on a perfect summer day.

A strange bird call joined the regulars.
Today must be a day for newcomers.
After late night's dream, what's next?

In my dream I am at a train station
with a little boy about three. The last
two train cars were small red motorcycles.

The boy in the last car offered the child
with me to ride on the other red bike.
His parents agree he can ride it.

These were American tracks- poorly maintained,
not the slick European trains.
I feared for the boy's safety as the train started.

To protect the boy's safety, I draped my body
over the bike from trip's bumps and splatters.
I was a much more flexible granny than real life.

I did not know where we were or where
we were going. I was not sure exactly
who these people were as we took off.

Soon the situation morphed into being
inside a metal container, packed like
the immigrants found in back of truck.

A small white dog replaced the boy and squeezed
between the passengers until the door opens.
I un-pretzel and exit with the dog.

I come upon a stack of envelopes with a band
around it saying "knowing". Unopened, I awake
and the clock says 555- an angel number.

The dream seems a collage of images from
the news and from decisions I have been contemplating.
I will have to research meaning of 555.

Probably the train was from considering rail
going East for the Women's March in DC
and to Connecticut in the fall–disregarded.

The concern over train infrastructure
from a news item, not enough track for new
fast track trains ordered? Maybe Musk's plan?

The metal container was not big enough
for a train car and no accommodations--
more like the immigrant truck tragedy.

Boy to dog weird. Agile granny weird also.
The unopened envelopes with hope of knowing--
disappointing. Still in cloud of unknowing.

My hope is in meaning of 555. I march inside
to research angel numbers. The birds caw
and wind chimes clink–goodbye.

555

Angel Number 555: Huge changes are unfolding throughout all areas of your life according to Divine will. The message however is not to sit back and be a passive recipient. It is a call from the universe and the angels to choose yourself and co-create positive change and blessings in your life now. Ask-Angels.com

I'm double-dipping chi today
by returning to the backyard
to focus on the message of 555.

I went inside to research the significance
of seeing 555 on my clock after waking
from a strange dream. What am I to do?

Since there are big changes in the air,
I need to do energy clearing, perhaps
past life clearing work to align with my soul purpose.

The goal is to raise to a higher vibration,
reveal new codes of light by quieting mind,
heart, third eye. A little chi might help.

Big changes bring a lot of unknowns,
555 indicates positive changes with greater
love, vitality and abundance.

Angels and guides support focusing
on my intentions, maintaining a high vibration,
even raising my vibration. I need to align.

555 is the energy of change, so release
the past fears and patterns that no longer serve.
Make way for a lighter, more uplifting patterns.

555 is about life choices to serve my path
and purpose. Express my truth, freedom,
authentic vibrations. Hope I rise to the challenge.

This call to positively change in an uplifting
and empowering way in a time of accelerated change
is one I resonate with and hope angels guide me.

I need to let go and refocus on infinite possibility,
so I can naturally align with divinely inspired
positive change. We need all the help we can get.

I need to stay present in the moment,
utilize affirmations and prayer to stay positive
and focus with the highest positive changes.

I'm assured I am well-equipped to handle
whatever changes are coming and hugely
supported by angels and guides.

Well, I pray nightly for angels to tug out
the black threads of negative energy, to surround
me with light as I explore the cosmos.

I write my gratitude journal, play with my muse,
have my chakras cleared by my masseuse.
But she is on vacation for two weeks.

I will have to rely on my angels and guides,
maybe longer sessions gathering chi.
My watchband is broken, so I'll intuit time.

I see several areas of darkness to enlighten.
I could be sitting out here an awful long time
to tackle these issues-- need to stay in shade.

At the moment I feel lunch pangs, prods
to nap- perhaps dream a clearer dream.
Aligning will definitely take some work.

Blueberries

Our blueberry shrub is abundant.
Quarts of organic blueberries in our fridge--
extra doses on my morning yogurt.

I try to buy organic local blueberries
when I can, but sometimes they come
from faraway and perhaps not too pristine.

But for now their white-grey bloom is blooming
on backyard berries and providing bellyfuls for me.
Also good with dark chocolate, anytime.

Research says blueberries have anti-oxidants
which help overall health and immune system.
As I nibble at them, they supposedly....

boost immune system, neutralize free radicals,
improve memory, maintain good eyesight,
lower cholesterol levels, prevent heart disease,

prevent urinary tract infections, cancer, constipation,
improve digestion, reduce belly fat, slow aging process,
act as natural anti-depressant and regulate blood sugar.

Blueberries might help me in some areas better
than others like belly fat, but I'll take whatever
benefits I can get. Blueberries rock as well as roll.

Mindfulness Meditation

Much of Buddhism can be boiled down to bad news/good news story. The bad news is that life is full of suffering and we humans are full of illusions. The good news is that these two problems are actually one problem. If we could get rid of our illusions–if we could see the world clearly–our suffering would end.
Robert Wright

Perhaps if I went into the backyard and could learn
mindfulness meditation, my forays gathering chi
would clarify my perspective and not sap energies.

But I can't help noticing and listening, paying
attention as the dead cherry tree goes bald,
as creatures scurry to their own destinies.

Apparently world-wide, people practice
mindful meditation to change perspectives
on feelings of anxiety, rage and to empower.

Our warped vision makes us suffer.
(Oops–a plane disrupts my plane of thought.)
Oh yes, evolutionary psychology gives thumbs up.

So I guess I just need to learn to get clarity.
The Buddhists' meditation is an exercise
in attention, calming mind, focusing on breath.

This results in equanimity to observe things
with unusual care and clarity–like sounds,
physical sensations, anything in field of awareness.

I guess I am not calm enough or breathing right.
I do pay attention, but feelings guide our perceptions,
thoughts and behavior not just careful observation.

Mindfulness calls for skepticism toward feelings.
I must critically inspect and decide which feelings
to trust says evolutionary psychology.

Apparently natural selection is indifferent
whether we are happy or sad, enlightened
or deluded–it is a blind process, not conscious designer?

Anxiety can be natural, grounded in our genes?
Maybe to make sure copies of our genes are safe?
But does natural selection really care?

We've developed social anxiety as well as survival
anxieties. People worry too much about what others
think of them and their offspring? Peer pressure?

Anxieties increased as our nature evolved
and environment changed. Buddhists emphasize
being aware of feelings and being less governed by them.

Achieving calm objectivity might help us deal?
Apparently tanha or cravings are an illusion
of enduring gratification. (I like jolts of dark chocolate.)

We look for the next gratifying thing. But dukkha
translates as unsatisfactoriness, not just suffering.
So we need to undermine our cravings.

Unfortunate illusions include misconceptions
of self that we think of being at our core. So we
misconceive nature of world, implanted agenda.

Great– we don't see world as it actually is
and no guarantees of happiness. We're duped.
Buddhist sized up the human predicament.

Mindfulness meditation could be a way
to address the problem. But if we are
in a holographic universe–what controls lens?

How can we correct our eyesight, control
our sensory input, achieve nirvana?
As I sit in the shade, I doubt I'll see the light.

Undermining Mindfulness

Mindfulness is the gateway into full dimensionality of being human.
Jon Kabat-Zinn

When I went into the backyard to contemplate
(meditate sounds like too advanced a term)
and to siphon some chi, I was surrounded by sound.

Mourning doves cooed to other bird chirps,
their chattering shattering my focus.
Wind-chimes clanged erratically.

Wind whishes leaves and shadows shift.
Butterflies fly bush to bush, but do not stay.
I spot a twitching gray tail.

On the wheelbarrow ramp from bottom
to top of sidewalk chunk wall, a squirrel
sprawls- splat gray on gray.

Still as a yard sculpture, he blends in so few
would notice he was there. I can't name him Frisky
after a squirrel in a poem I wrote at six.

But who am I to chastise his snooze, as I sit
like a chunk of blue cheese, hopefully
imbibing chi energy through black SAS shoes?

I am reminded what I am sitting here to ponder.
While munching lunch, I watched Oprah interview:
Jon Kabat-Zinn on Mindfulness.

To him life becomes a meditation when you seek
a moment of peace at home. Mindfulness blends
art and science--ways of knowing the world.

He states as long as you are breathing, there is
more right with you, than what is wrong with you,
no matter what is wrong with you.

You are to pour enough into what is right with you.
Be present, discover who you are. Breathe deep
into the calmness beneath your unruly mind.

That seemed a lot to chew before I went outside
to focus on what's inside me. I breathe deeply,
but keep my eyes open. I believe I'm multi-dimensional.

The squirrel decides to scamper up a tree after
a few ground nibbles and stays there a few minutes
out of my sight range, hidden in canopy.

Then the squirrel ambles along the top of the wall,
forays to lawn looking for morsels,
tummies tidbits. He sparks my intention.

Undeterred by siren or sight of me
the squirrel is steadfast in his quest.
I'll call him Sparkles.

After all my distractions, I return to contemplation
of what mindfulness could do for our complex,
turbulent world, scrambling for meaning.

Sparkles and I are two backyard creatures
gathering energy to move forth
in the mid-afternoon sun, mindfully or not.

Feeding on Chi

A squirrel pokes his head over the roof-line
contemplating taking a leap to the nearest branch.
A spider has a hanging bridge between trees.

The squirrel hesitates, goes out of sight,
then leaps to a lower limb of the blue spruce,
to the fence and to the neighbor's roof.

He bypasses a wide-array of numerous
filberts and windfall apples splayed before me.
The nutshells indicate others liked our fare.

Butterflies and birds scout out our organic,
pesticide-free produce. Other times the squirrels
join in, but today this squirrel went elsewhere.

As I absorb Gaia's and cosmic chi, I recall
when a healer in 2014 told me to connect to chi
in my backyard to heal. It was autumn.

I rose at sunrise, grabbed my mother's red cape
for warmth and sat on an uncomfortable cane/stool,
then a more comfortable camp chair.

I did this for about a year in fair-weather and inside
looking out when damp or too cold. I wrote
Red Cape Capers: Playful Backyard Meditations.

This time a massage therapist told me to ground
my root chakra and promote healing by
re-connecting with chi. It is summer.

I have a new metal chair and side table replacing
the camp chair. I do not need a cape and sit in
the shade, later in the day for contemplation.

I am not sure how long I will do this. I am writing
a book, which if I include chi poems might make
two books–alter my concept for the poetry collection.

Meanwhile birds and squirrels harvest filberts
instead of cherries. Cracked shells instead of pits
swept into compost. Feeding frenzy continues.

The Harvester

Here I am, Granny Smith sitting
amid Delicious and MacIntosh apples.
Two grafted varieties did not thrive.

The windfalls are devotedly wrapped
in newspaper, boxed and stored
in my husband's shed.

Worms and scales do not matter,
they can be cored out. He slices
apples into salads, tops cereals.

He harvested cherries before
it was borer-ed to death.
Filbert snacks last all year.

Blueberry bushes picked.
Blue balls bounce on yogurt,
salads, cereals and snacked.

Rarely a plum or peach.
He used to graze the greens
in one phase for natural dining.

His crops are all pesticide-free.
We don't poison other creatures
who share our yard's bounty.

This Granny Smith feeds on chi.
Only the blueberries bounce
in her belly.

Things Are Heating Up

Today it is supposed to go over 100.
Three days of perhaps 106-108 degrees.
I need to get my stints with chi early.

After exercise, getting groceries,
a quick e-mail check, I grabbed
some dark chocolate. I'm out there by 11.

Where is everyone?
A few birdcalls- mourning doves,
screechers and one sounds like a duck.

Apples fall on shadow-dappled lawn.
Nutshells crunch underfoot.
But no one is taking the bait.

Perhaps too early for squirrels
and birds to munch lunch.
No picky eaters today?

Perhaps they huddle under bushes,
flap their wings to cool off.
Only a few birds and butterflies here.

Car murmurations in the distance.
One plane without much sound or contrail.
No motor mowers sweating today.

Wind rustles wind-chimes
enough breeze to cool.
Enough shade to be comfortable.

I do not need a hat or sun lotion
for my brief moments of attempted
meditation, yet my mind roils.

There is a lot I could get hot under
my collar about (if I had one) on
so many levels and distances.

I choose to stay calm, cool and collected,
think about air-conditioned afternoon,
before going out to dinner.

There is so much to get hot and bothered about,
I should treasure the muted sounds
and sheltering from heat.

I eat the dark chocolate before it melts.
The taste lingers as I go inside to prepare lunch.
Will the backyard creatures come–

before apples squish and mush into applesauce,
before morsels seem micro-waved,
before heat lessens their appetite?

Heat Wave

At 11 it is 88 degrees,
twenty more expected
later in the day.

I go directly to the backyard
after exercise class to
beat the heat.

On my twenty-minute watch
not one bird or squirrel
landed in the yard.

The weak wind can't flush
the inversion layer heavy with forest
fire smoke from the valley.

A few mourning doves in next yard.
Wimpy ding of wind chimes.
Not even a butterfly.

An apple drops nearby.
A quick count estimates about 30
windfalls waiting for pick up.

There is a bucket of filberts
inside the door, so maybe creatures
think we have lean pickings.

Three huge fans in the small exercise room
lead to discussions of possible power failures
as have occurred elsewhere due to heat.

In July our home lost power three times-
twice with cars crashing poles and once
with a crow fried in a transformer.

We have momentary-to-hours-long glitches
which mean re-setting clocks, reading
by flashlight. But today–I hope power holds on

like the lower limb solo apple clinging
to a spindly branchlet, gently waving.
Daily I check to see if it hung on.

All the shades in the house are drawn.
Skylights brighten some rooms.
I'll microwave chicken piece for lunch.

Last night I watched a documentary
on Thomas Edison, the Wizard of Menlo Park
who electrified the world with his gadgets.

It was not too long ago we did not have
cooling convenience on these hot days.
We forget how pampered we are.

All exercise crones concerned about the heat,
while I was pondering the latest blunders
in the newspapers boiling my temper.

No matter how hot it gets today inside
or outside of me, I need to cool down,
hydrate and meditate calm.

My Refuge Field

Should I go back outside
in the sweltering heat to build
a Refuge Field?

The Tibetan Buddhist meditation
to envision all my teachers and their lineages
starts with a clear blue sky.

Well, this afternoon is smoggy,
sky grayish and smoky. Not suitable
for such an extensive task.

While constructing this spiritual
family tree, so I feel supported in my work,
I should see a mentor appear.

Maybe from the V's and Ws of my mini-orchard
trunk crotches, the branching limbs and leaves
could evoke and symbolize my family tree?

Trying it inside with writer friends,
I came up with May Swenson
and before May, my mother...so far.

My mother encouraged my creativity
as I explored various branches
of human endeavors.

May Swenson is like a kindred spirit,
experimental poet, Swedish heritage, same curiosity,
rebellious, boundary breaker instincts.

Is she my objective correlative to bounce
my ideas from? She pondered and wondered about
many branches of knowledge and the unknown also.

I peer out the window at the backyard's
sun-shimmer. Cool, I decided to abandon
interior musing until conditions seem more conducive.

State of Emergency

Smoke from wildfires could stick around in the Willamette Valley until Friday. The smoke could keep temperatures a few degrees cooler. This is because the smoke is thick enough to block some sunlight from getting through. A powerful high-pressure system arrived just at the height of summer. Weather Service

Hot, hazy, hazardous out-
I heave heavy air. The Governor
calls a state of emergency.

Wildfires' smoke from Canada
and Mt. Jefferson invade the valley.
The elderly and young should stay inside.

No strenuous outside exercise. Well,
I'm a crone, but just sitting should
not keep me from my daily chi.

In cloudless blue/gray sky
a plane fuzzes as if in fog.
Neighbor's yard blurs.

The birds are less chatty,
but not coughing. A bee
sways on the solo dandelion.

It's murky, smelly, thick air
like city air pollution. Stagnant
air until at least tomorrow.

I do not feel I'm getting much benefit
sitting here inhaling unhealthy air,
but chi probably not effected.

Another over 100 degree day expected.
The county fair has few attendees
and vendors sell mostly cold drinks.

Tonight Bard in the Quad will play
Shakespeare outside. Usually it's
chilly with ocean winds–not tonight

Community events will suffer.
Asthmatics will breathe harder.
Weed-free day if gardeners are not early.

I sit and contemplate morning news
of wasteful, foolish government decisions:
wall, new immigration laws, de-funding services.

Our Oregon governor called state of emergency
to mobilize resources as needed for firefighting.
Oregon has red-flag, critical fire danger.

The declaration will ensure state agencies
have the needed resources to minimize
the impact of the wildfires. Open cooling centers.

In Washington DC there seems a national
state of emergency in leadership
and responsibility to all citizens.

Should I mope in the shade, sneeze
or go inside, hydrate, cool, clear my mind--
try to decide what I actually can control?

Reality

Reality is fragile. If we intend to share it with one another, we have an
obligation to protect it. And that's one big reason that art is always teaching us.
The more familiar we become with what reality isn't, the better we understand
it...Parsing our dreams teaches us how to separate what's real from what's
unknowable. As imaginative beings, exercising that literacy is one of life's
greatest pleasures. As citizens, it's suddenly become one of our greatest
responsibilities. Chris Richards

Yesterday Portland reached 106 degrees
with pollution higher than Beijing.
Reality was baking on concrete.

Yesterday Corvallis reached 104 degrees.
Today smoke lessens, winds stronger.
Reality will toast us into the 90s.

The politicians taking a reality break?
Fake or real news cycle taking a time out?
Facing constituents, politicians could get roasted.

What is real for me in my backyard plunk down,
is no companions- just bird-shadows, puffballs,
even windfall apples picked up. Nutshells raked.

No stragglers holding heads high above
the uniform-cut lawn. Coos of mourning doves,
moan of a train whistle–out of sight.

Is reality an illusion? Possible to know?
Dreams teachable and reachable?
I'll ponder inside where it is cooler.

How much does our biological heritage
influence our perception of reality?
How much do our decisions–or flukes?

A Portland woman who thought she was an Irish
Catholic found out from a DNA test she was half
European Jewish, Middle Eastern and Eastern European.

Her father an orphan was switched at birth
in the hospital and his destiny and reality altered.
He grew up not knowing his true identity.

The complications for the descendants
and how they chose to deal with the reality
raised many questions.

My questions about my biological heritage
are few–pure Swedish for endless generations.
Four grandparents emigrated as youths.

One great-grandfather impregnated two women.
Minister told him to marry one and pay off the other.
He married my grandmother's mother. Paid off other.

The discarded son Sven was abandoned by grandparents
at 14, became part of the farm labor system, read widely,
changed name to become Sven Vallare –a published poet.

Our mutual great-grandfather recited sagas from memory,
shared love of poetry with my grandmother, Clara.
She immigrated, Sven stayed. Never knew each other.

Sven was told his father immigrated to America. Clara
was told her father's love child was sent to Europe
with the mother–false. Father drank and gambled inheritance.

Clara's father married a healthy peasant as his wealthy
family declined and he was left with a small farm to work.
How would Sven and Clara's lives been different if they knew?

All shared love of poetry. So did my mother's mother.
So plenty of inherited tendency toward poetry?
My Swedish relatives found and embraced Sven's family.

My husband's ancestors came over on the Mayflower,
William Pye, the worst Poet Laureate of England
was his relative–lots of English, Irish, German.

So our son is half Swedish and half Irish, English, German.
His children reduced to 1/4 Swedish and other fractions.
But how much reality is body and how much mind?

Our daughter is adopted with several fractions unknown.
Her son's father gave him Italian, French etc.
Our ties are not biological, yet we share a reality.

For me, my body is the vehicle perhaps I chose before
I incarnated to fulfill my life chart and purpose I came for.
All the bio-baggage coding impinges on my reality?

I expect my soul energy and consciousness may inhabit
many physical and non-physical forms in many places
as energy and consciousness seem to be eternal?

For now I experience reality—as difficult as it can be
to understand and accept in this fleshy form. I parse
my dreams as best I can to explore and question reality.

At this fragile reality moment, I am grateful to be inside,
cool, in un-smudged air of my beloved Oregon. My reality
is often beyond my grasp, yet I am responsible to hold it?

Writing poetry is a great pleasure, I try to take
responsibility for all aspects of my reality, but find
many breaks, hot patches beyond my control.

Your Dancing Place

Take earth for your large room and the floor of earth carpeted with sunlight and
hung with silver wind for your dancing place. May Swenson

Windfall apples fell abundantly this weekend.
The apple and hazelnut trees' branches intertwine
wrestling for sunlight as if dancing.

These are sturdy trees in summer-hardened clay.
Elsewhere drunk trees topple as permafrost
melts with climate change, lose their grip.

In an hour I leave for a memorial service,
to support my friend of a happy couple
who is left behind to grieve.

The dead cherry tree awaits its chop down.
Beige leaves fall. Birds look for berries elsewhere.
We will miss the bird battles for the cherries.

Blueberries fructify, birds fly by,
butterflies swirl, squirrels scamper,
graceful movements in life's dance.

For the precious time we are here,
Earth sustains us. Moon inspires us.
This is the place we dance our lives.

In the Eyes of the Beholder

Art washes away the dust of everyday life.   Pablo Picasso

Three apples plopped before me in my chi time.
Several blue jays pecked at filberts,
cracking nuts on branches.

The heat wave is cooling, so I expected
more action, more feeders.
Little bird chatter. Few butterflies flit.

But bugs buzz. Two fuzzy flowers
near the wall stiffly wave in the wind.
Close to the wall they escaped mower.

They are white-headed. Puffballs of clover
or dandelions? Maybe mysterious plants
from seeds, free from the fair booth?

They look like moons. Perhaps
they have a moon-ly name?
White-gray heads like hubby and me.

I decide I will rickety-over to guess
their name. But the uneven ground
deters me. Probably could not name them.

My vision is blurred. Probably cataracts.
My glasses tint darker in the warm sun.
Yard looks like a late Monet.

Part of the pleasure of the yard is its design,
craggy wall, canopies, spots of color,
birds, flowers, fruit and creatures.

In the hubbub of the day, my un-dusted house
is redeemed by its artistic flares, walls
and surfaces covered with imagination.

Inside or outside my aging eyes delight
at the hues of views, textures to touch.
Art enhances the quotidian.

Ode to Our Cherry Tree

When I wasn't home, they chopped you down,
leaving a jumble of stumps to move.
No more cherries. No pit-litter-- Now.
a spotlight of sun between pear and filbert trees.

Leaving a jumble of stumps to move,
onto the woodpile to await burning.
A spotlight of sun between pear and filbert trees,
no longer do your shadows mingle.

Onto the woodpile to await burning–
perhaps you'll provide creatures shelter?
No longer do your shadows mingle.
No more bite-battles between birds and people.

Perhaps you'll provide creatures shelter?
Our nets, shiny pans detours gone.
Your red cherries gleamed in sun.
attracting a place for respite and appetite.

Our nets, shiny pan detours gone.
No more ladders to press your trunk.
Attracting a place for respite and appetite,
you remained organic until sprayed last year.

No more ladders to press your trunk.
We noticed your vibrancy decline.
You remained organic until sprayed last year.
We shared with birds your last harvest.

We noticed your vibrancy decline,
aging like us over thirty years.
You grew taller. Cherries harder to reach.
When your leaves turned prematurely beige—we knew.

Aging like us over thirty years
our days of cherished cherries were over.
When your leaves turned prematurely beige, we knew.
You leave a sunny patch in the yard.

Our days of cherished cherries were over.
No more cherries. No pit-litter now.
You leave a sunny patch in our yard.
When I wasn't home, they chopped you down.

Restless Nutcrackers

A squirrel cracks filberts against branch,
scrambles and dangles, feast in hand.
A stellar jay causes an avalanche
of leaves and nuts out of command.

Squirrel scampers to sun-hardened ground.
Stellar jay struggles in foliage until nut cracked.
Both have to scurry, scuttle around
until nut finds snackers to attract.

Aloft or aground they clutch a nut.
Both litter shells on sun-baked earth.
On same tree, their limbs don't abut,
then they scatter to another berth.

They dine without conversation,
silently crunch and munch tidbits.
Perhaps telepathic communication
as they travel in their own orbits?

Handling the Remnants

The stumps from the cherry tree chop down
line the side of the garage–firewood lengths,
awaiting pick-up by our daughter.

I was unprepared to see the empty ground.
It looked like a recent burial mound,
a wound to the grass.

They cut below the lawn level, chipped the remains.
My husband raked soil over the barren ground.
He filled the hole, smoothed the gape.

At three the shadow of the hazelnut tree
sprawled over the spot the cherry tree
once covered with canopy.

Birds peck the filbert nuts free,
scatter leaves and shells.
Windfall apples are gathered and stored.

Through bird-chatter, do they know
their organic cherry tree is gone?
Their choices apples and nuts?

The peach tree has produced one.
The blueberries are lean pickings.
But the apples are super-abundant.

Our grandson wants us to plant another
cherry tree. When he comes to visit
and sees the bare spot, will he be sad?

It takes a long time to grow a cherry tree.
Will we be here to harvest cherries
even if we plant right now?

Why didn't the birds dig deep enough
to eat the borers? The tree was stressed.
Now we all are.

Nimbus of Nakedness

Watching the birds crackling on branches,
are they nude or are feathers
considered their clothing?

What about apples?
Are they naked or only naked
under their skin?

In exercise class nudity came up
in context of loincloth exposures
at an upcoming powwow.

Or at the Oregon Country Fair
where a newcomer was warned
there were a lot of naked fair-goers.

These crones seemed to get flushed
and excited at the prospect
as they had no mates at home.

Our whole family went to the Country Fair
for several years. It was the time when sun-kissed
kids were named, Rainbow, Sunshine, Cloud.

People flashed naked or with costumes
festooned with feathers, face paint, strategic
tattoos–undressed walking art statements.

I loved the artistic crafts, earthy
atmosphere, sustainability exhibits,
mini-plays–even Shakespeare.

One year one of our children protested:
Why we were bringing them into
such a pot-filled, unclad den?

I still chuckle at the unadorned band.
Instruments held high, swaying
penises and breasts along a forest path.

I have not been for decades- never nude.
Now can't hike shady paths. No one would
want to see me without abundant covering.

The Rusty Angel

Carry out a random act of kindness, safe in the knowledge that one day someone might do the same for you. Diana, Princess of Wales

A crow-size rusting metal angel
blows her horn, flies under a branch
of the heavy-laden, hazelnut tree.

A few thin limbs needed to be snipped
before she can take flight with wind,
hang out with birds bustling beside her.

Animal art in the front yard.
Angel art in the backyard–
a solid symbol to go with the flow.

She camouflages well with birds
and squirrels. They might be surprised
especially when she wind-wiggles.

All the animal art creatures have names.
I will call this angel, Airlika.
She is airy and I like her.

Airlika was a gift from a longtime friend
who knows I collect angels and she
was moving. Airlika will evoke memories.

The same day, the backyard added
other gifts–a bird feeder and a high-pitched
wind-chime dangling CD's to catch wind.

Now the angel will have two wind-chimes
of different tones along with birdsong
for accompaniment as she toots her horn.

The bird house is without birdseed.
The trees nourish the birds now, but
year-round Airlika has winged-ones near.

As long as I inspirit chi in the backyard,
attempt to meditate, an inspiring angel
reminds me, though even rusty, I can uplift.

The Rain Returns

Two things stand like a stone, kindness in another's trouble, and courage in your
own. Diana, Princess of Wales

A gentle rain beads bubbles on my metal chair,
pings on leaves, light drumbeats on the shed.
No shadows, no squirrels, no birds.

I wipe off the chair with my hand
it is still wet. It is quite warm so
I figure I will let body heat dry me.

The rain sprinkles hands and knees.
I move the chair under drier eave,
between the wheelbarrow and shed.

Moist scenery seems a shade darker.
More like when shade darkens.
This is my first rainy chi day in the backyard.

Water drips from lips of concrete-chunk
wall. Cherry tree's grave site moistened.
Heavy air and gray sky dampens.

Airlika angel's rust a deeper copper.
No breeze for the wind chimes.
A more somber mood prevails.

Yesterday the bully-bluster of Trump
aimed at North Korea, not at the White
Nationalists, who car-rammed their opponents.

Months of stress leave the nation overwhelmed.
Dangerous and unpredictable leadership,
requires kindness and courage from us all.

With the mourning doves cooing
in the distance, this could be a vigil
for demise of light leading up to solar eclipse.

Not an apple fell. Not a rustling in leaves.
A stray raindrop taps my hand. I dream
for sunny days to return.

Flashes of light

Flashes of light dash down the hallway.
A sputtering fairy? A flickering night light?
I approached the open door gingerly to peek.

It was an early morning bathroom run
when I discovered sparklers. The night light
was not the culprit. Fairy—maybe?

My husband explained it was sun-rays
gleaming off CDs he added to wind-chimes
to help them catch wind, sparkling through a window.

It was cloudy when he installed them,
so he was startled when the flashes
came into his office and dazzled hall walls.

CDs were not effective against birds
when they dangled from the cherry branches,
or as a deer deterrent fencing side yards.

These sparklers dim in shade quickly.
By the time I sit in the backyard,
they are barely shiny under the eaves.

But these CDs do induce sound.
The wind tinkles them even when
they don't twinkle in sun.

The cherry tree and deer are gone.
Recycling CDs for light-flashes
and high-pitched chimes—delights.

Thinking about Charlottesvile

I am thinking about the people who came out to stand up against hate, and I am
thinking about the angry faces and hate I saw on so many people who came from
out of town to spread hate and anger. And it is frightening. Rene Balfour

As I sit in the sunny backyard after rain:
no smoke, clear sky, slight chill,
I think of Unite the Right rally in Charlottesville.

When protesters against hate groups faced them,
a car driven by a Nazi sympathizer mowed down crowd,
killing one woman and injuring many others.

Two police in a helicopter crash died.
Why didn't the police do more to prevent violence?
Cars have been used in terrorist attacks elsewhere.

At first the President did not denounce the hate groups,
(many his supporters) to the outrage of many who feel
his election empowered these fascist, hate groups.

Days later Trump finally speaks out against hate groups, but
nationally anti-hate groups already set up vigils and protests
even stopping rightist rally leader from a press conference.

People held candles, flowers, balloons and signs: Make racists
ashamed again. No hate. No fear. Everyone is welcome here.
No Trump! No KKK! No fascist USA! Black lives Matter.

In the name of humanity we refuse
to accept a fascist America sums up
what the vast majority believes.

This division, anger, hate in part is because
Trump did not receive the popular vote
and his policies are not in the best interest of America.

This unrest will continue as he engenders fear in his stance
against North Korea, against climate change, against corruption,
sound immigration and travel, education, health care etc.

The list is long and the public's patience turns to worry
as he seems to lack competence and mental stability.
One week until the solar eclipse crosses the nation. Omen?

Through back fence slats, I see my neighbor nourishes
a large swaying dandelion crop. At present we have just one bloom.
When will the weeds invade our yard? Spread like hate?

Rally for Charlottesville
White silence=White consent: sign at Rally for Charlottesville at Corvallis, Oregon

It is overcast with stray rain-spit as I gather
chilly chi slumped in a chair in the backyard. I am
near tears with revulsion at Charlottesville's tragedy.

The repulsive racial and religious hate rally
received condemnation around the world
and delayed response from Trump.

More than 500 people gathered at the courthouse
at 6 in Corvallis, to stand for what is upright, civil, kind,
against hate in our college town like Charlottesville.

Two women from Now organized the spur
of the moment rally on Facebook. Other groups
like NAACP joined in. Concerned individuals.

The crowd was encouraged to respond to racism
and intolerance with love. This was a peaceful
demonstration–no weapons. We must teach love.

One speaker said we must stay strong and stand
together to turn violence away. Not with violence.
Violence begets violence. Start with some gun laws?

Chalk messages and signs support diversity.
Many signs have seen many marches.
The majority does not want what Trump empowers.

Imagine the WW2 veterans seeing Nazi flags
and Nazi supporters they fought to quell.
The KKK did not even cover up.

Trump has a Jewish daughter and son-in-law.
David Duke of KKK praises Trump's agenda.
Angry white males mourn loss of white privilege.

A Nazi ran over a white young woman in Charlottesville.
How many deranged white men will continue to attack
churches, schools, Blacks, women, public places?

Freedom of speech carries responsibility.
Hate speech is not tolerated in many countries.
Unite the Right gang had weapons-ready to fight.

Dahleen Glaxton suggests insecure white males
blame their social and economic failures
on everyone but themselves, escalate bigotry.

White males fear they are losing the unfair advantage
they enjoyed since nation's founding by disenfranchising
women, Native Americans, Blacks, immigrants.

The wealth inequities, mostly white greed produced,
breeds discontent and in time revolution?
99% not getting basic needs funds might get pissed.

Why did the displaced workers think billionaire Trump
cared about them? He did not pay all his workers,
has overseas assets, won't reveal taxes.

He appeals to bigots, under-educated,
poor, desperate people. Obama appealed to hope.
Trump to intolerance, bullying and greed.

America is not just for white men to exploit.
We have been enriched by women, Blacks,
and immigrants– contributions from all backgrounds

I sit here shivering with frustration and fear.
Tiki-torches emblazoned angry faces.
Social media exposed them. Many lost jobs.

Hope is in the anti-hate rallies across the country.
How many rallies and marches will it take? Daily
Trump tweets and acts against Constitution, decency.

I don't want to sit by and watch the USA crumble
because we do not impeach a mentally-ill President,
who did not receive popular vote and is low in polls.

I watch our lone dandelion fluff white, ready to puff
seeds by the wind. I dream of winds of change
when seeds plant diverse, sustainable, healthy growth.

Healing with Angels

We become writers not because we have a story to tell, and not even because we have talent. It's because we have a wound that we are constantly in need of trying to heal. Chris Abani

Airlika, my rusty, horn-blowing metallic angel
cradles under the limb of a hazelnut tree,
weathers whatever comes, encrusts.

Now protected by canopy's shade,
lush leaves, dangling nuts, soon she will be
exposed to rain and cold—stand out, vulnerable.

Angels supposedly heal, inspire, guide us
through the turmoil and tumult of Earthly life.
I have to believe in angels to hack this realm.

My mother stitched needlework of me in a cradle
surrounded by angels. Girls contend with fear,
sexism, violence and injustice. I was wounded.

My long blonde hair cast me as an angel
in Christmas pageants. Later when my son died,
I began surrounding myself with thousands of angels.

Each life seems to endure wounds and I
do not understand why this is necessary
in a world whose supposed goal is love.

Duality is not the reality I want to live in.
We are walking wounded until dead. Trying
to enlighten in this dimmed world is relentless.

If we can imagine a better life why can't we create it?
Does free will need so much damaging negativity?
Raise the vibration! Time for a light-takeover!

I write my wound of trying to understand Gaia
and our place in the cosmos. The pain I witness
and feel makes my heart-wound pound.

I rely on angels to uplift, help me serve
a higher purpose, diminish darkness.
I need to feel and heal from their light.

Something hurts, and the wound that it has left is so incredibly painful and so present that we have no other choice but to write out of that wound.
Tameka Cage Conley

Bugged

I say YES to being a better receiver. Louise Hay

Yesterday when sitting in the backyard for chi,
a lean, iridescent, about two-inch, blue bug
landed on a windfall apple near me.

It required long lapses between flights.
It flicked its wings but stayed mostly
stationary. Then a series of loops.

Several trips orbited the apple,
then a leap to another apple
and a third before home apple.

It danced around amid flies, bees,
butterflies. Other insects seemed
oblivious as the blue bug solo carried on.

During Scrabble a friend looked up
blue bugs for me on her cell, but
none looked like my blue bug.

Today several bees grazed the apples.
They did not stay in the area but seconds.
Finally my blue bug returned to the same apple.

But this time it was a brief, non-loopy visit
and it took off to the wall. Was this
bug a cosmic messenger? If so, what?

I feel ravens and crows might be
relatives checking on me–but a blue bug?
I had not seen this bug in all my observations.

Perhaps it is a blue dragonfly? When I go in
I will research blue dragonflies. Do they have
a certain cosmic significance?

But a bee buzzed my head- circling
persistently until I went inside. Was
this an annoyed messenger? Fly friend?

In any case, tomorrow I will look
for my beautiful, blue bug and wonder
how lucky I am our paths crossed.

Spirit of the Dragonfly

My blue bug is indeed a blue dragonfly,
a symbol of transformation. I researched
websites for dragonfly symbolism.

Somehow I intuited the dragonfly
was a symbol to pay attention too,
to learn about and reflect upon.

The spirit of a dragonfly suggests
moving past self-created illusions
that generally limit growth and change.

The spirit of the dragonfly means renewal,
a positive force and power of life in general.
I am trying to get its chi and change.

To Native Americans is a power of light,
swiftness and activity, pure water, renewal
in a time of great hardship.

In Japan, called Land of Dragonflies, they are
a symbol of courage, strength and happiness-
appear in art, literature and haiku.

For me, an Oregon crone, the spirit of dragonflies
can be helpful in dealing with addictions–like
over-eating. Oh no–not dark chocolate!

The spirit of dragonfly symbolizes leaving behind
old beliefs of powerlessness, irrational fears
and false limitations. A pivotal point with energy.

Take full responsibility for what we make of life
and make changes. One has the energy and support
and power of spirit of dragonflies. Reflect and attract.

Call on the spirit of dragonflies by focusing on rainbow
colors for your aura via universal flow. Colors can be
for healing if you absorb and retain dragonfly energy.

The spirit of dragonflies can clear lower chakras
and stir trapped energies which can manifest
throughout our body if not released.

We can infuse our lower chakras with clear,
brilliant colors. The spirit of dragonflies
supports you through this clearing process.

The spirit of dragonflies strips away beliefs
of containment of our actions, our limitations,
our doubts and self-doubts. Everything is possible.

With the spirit of dragonflies we can achieve
dreams and goals, learn and understand ourselves.
Dragonflies are keepers of dreams.

Imagine we can see our true potential and ability,
fulfill our birthright, increase our intuitive ability and
connect to the universe with shades of blue and indigo.

My dragonfly was blue and my favorite color.
We can use color to attract or deter messages
we send. Work with crystals and brightly infused stones.

Imagine we could be like a sparkling new dragonfly.
We could empower ourselves and fly daily with
a higher power of spirit, connecting with universal power.

Ah, to be free to follow paths from our inner self
to achieve, experience and follow dragonfly spirit
to help ourselves and others.

I hope my beloved blue dragonfly returns
as I work on my renewal and transformation,
maybe accelerated by the solar eclipse.

My massage therapist clears my chakras,
places warm stones and works on sore muscles.
The blue dragonfly affirms she was a good choice.

The first sighting on the apple, the loops and
leaps could have been my confusion. The second
brief visit suggests I could be ready for straight flight.

Whatever the spirit of dragonfly symbolizes–
a blue dragonfly is special, a hopeful sign
at some point I'll fly in the light direction.

The Best Spot

Two days before the solar eclipse
my husband and I scout the front
and back yards for the best viewing spot.

Holding cardboard, certified safe
eclipse glasses, we survey sun position
between nine and ten in the morning.

We study shadow patterns and try
to get solar glasses over our glasses
before sun rays blind us.

It is good we practiced as we did not
get glasses on quickly enough and did
get glints of sun in our eyes briefly.

The front yard driveway, stone wall,
sidewalk near street was a bit stark.
Maybe beside the yard art parade?

In the backyard a plum tree at west
fence and a peach tree at east with no
peachy or plum-ly partners cast shadows.

Center lawn are two apple and two
hazelnut trees with intertwining limbs
partnered and aligned to square dance.

Unpicked windfall apples pock the lawn.
Bees and a dragonfly speckle the apples,
flick about in the backyard dance.

The glasses really black out sun.
I stumble into what might be best spot,
stand and aim at sun. Aha—orange globe!

We can set up lawn chairs with blue table
between to hold our glasses. Maybe refreshments?
Sun tan lotion hopefully needed—no clouds or smoke.

We'll have to harvest the bug-bombed apples
if we want to keep insects at bay. The cherry
tree's burial mound—open ground-- might be it.

Umbraphiles

Honk 4 umbraphiles: Bumper sticker

Solar eclipse lovers stream
toward the path of totality across
the nation from all over the world.

Today is the day before the eclipse. Yesterday's
Oregon traffic was surprisingly lighter than expected.
But some roads clogged, wildfires, small plane crash.

Elsewhere 40,000 protesters in Boston opposed
racism. Other cities held protests. But in Corvallis,
we quietly prepared to celebrate the solar eclipse.

Today OSU 150 Space Grant Festival: a Total Eclipse
Festival will make sunprints, pet meteorites,
explore moon and stars, writing workshops, art.

Open Streets is another free street festival
giant-sized games, yoga, percussion jam,
bicycle-powered carnival rides, demonstrations.

My husband will bike to both events
as a volunteer and participant—I'll miss both
as well as a Solar Eclipse Festival: "Totality Inspired"

I will be car-bound, go into the backyard for chi,
watch birds and bug behavior which should shift
tomorrow at this time during the eclipse.

Windfall apples population exploded! One on chair.
Yard looks like it has measles. Bees flit about
apple to apple—overwhelmed by the bounty.

In hazelnut canopies various bird species
whack nuts against bark, carry tidbits away.
A red-topped, back and belly- white-striped stranger?

Newspapers proclaim fractured nation united
by the eclipse, suggest reflection during silence
and quiet for two minutes 39 seconds tomorrow.

Umbraphiles from all over the world gather
in Oregon. We are prepared for their visit.
Tomorrow should be clear skies. Welcome calm.

Operation Solar Eclipse

August 21, 2017 Starts 9:04 am. Ends 11:37 am.
Totality 10:17- 1 minute 39 seconds until midway 10:18 and 10:19.

Two chairs in front yard on driveway.
Two chairs in backyard near an apple tree.
Two pairs of solar glasses at each station.

My husband was photographing
and using his pinprick viewing device
he made, as well as solar glasses.

We had eclipse glasses over regular glasses
as the eclipse began. I stayed in the backyard
with apples plopping – Newton's gravity works.

He went back and forth taking many shots.
I wore my eclipse tee shirt and had a blanket
for when the temperature plunged with darkness.

Distractions–three scam calls–rudely received.
Contrail beneath the path of totality.
On the wall a spider web glistens in the sun.

While hubby gleefully hopped about,
I focused on the ten things lists–to release
and move into with the portal. Not sure they made it.

Scientists and volunteers fly and peer through telescopes
to learn more about the sun. Across the nation we are awed
by celestial coincidence, magical cosmic grandeur. Unified briefly.

Trump–ever the good example-- did not
wear protective glass and stared directly
into the sun. Why was I not surprised?

From a spiritual perspective: Sara Wiseman
suggests the eclipse signifies:
> Divine feminine (moon) will block divine masculine (sun).
> Emotion will block action.
> Intuition will block rationality.
> The inner will block the outer.

Both of us were prepared with glasses, reading,
lectures, eager to be present and discover
how we would react and feel as sun darkens.

I was facing east. The moon passes on a diagonal,
enter top right, exit bottom left. Like giant Pac-man
sun gobbling then upchucking the moon. Splash of pink.

The bites opened wider and wider. Orange slices
then almost two minutes of darkness and chill.
Breeze stronger. Birds cheep-less. Eerie quiet.

I sporadically watched the shifting light for two hours.
Listened to public radio for what to look for and what
was happening with eclipse and the visiting hordes.

I posed holding the white board for pinprick photos
after the brilliant, blinding flash of sun's return.
On science channel I saw events more clearly later.

I can understand how frightening an eclipse
could be to our ancestors and the myths they created
to explain such a dazzling, puzzling phenomenon.

I cannot report I felt overly emotional or intuitive.
Not sure my inner blocked my outer. I was curious,
intent on viewing clearly, processing the indescribable.

The Pacific Northwest had a solar eclipse March 26th, 1979.
The children went to school early. They were afraid kids
would look at the sun, but it was cloudy. Not that memorable.

Today was clear in the Willamette Valley and Central
Oregon, but foggy at the coast at first landfall. Air
and ground traffic resumed–engines raring to go.

Up to the eclipse, emergency preparations
and traffic snarls worked better than expected.
Not sure how thousands came and will leave.

Our operation solar eclipse finished, I went inside,
wiped off some sun screen, early lunch watching
eclipse repeat in a corner of tv screen. New Age coming?

I endeavored to be productive and take down spring
decorations mostly ducks and bunnies for Halloween
mostly witches and cats. Halloween needs more time to shine.

I'll conjure witches on broomsticks with familiar cat shadow
crossing the moon–solo woman thing, eclipsing darkness.
May the witch hunt in DC begin to bring things to light.

The Day After the Great American Eclipse

This is the first Total Solar Eclipse since our birth in 1776 which is visible only in the continental United States. For astrologers this has really amped concerns, predictions and imaginings for the possible ramifications of this Eclipse, especially for the U.S. Steffan Vanel

Yesterday we felt connected to something bigger,
part of a cosmic plan. People celebrated, partied
we cooperated, acted responsibly–mostly. Jubilant.

People patiently endured traffic delays, pulled
to side of road during totality, did not start wildfires.
People gathered from around the world peacefully.

Today I went into the same backyard, shaded
from directly seeing the sun. I did not see stars
or planets with the eclipse. Today it was smoky.

A solitary spider web thread dangled a tan
leaf like a cradle or ladle-- to rest or to eat?
Independent of wind, it spins pirouettes.

It sways, spirals, increases intensity
until a dervish. The choreography shifts
styles and pacing. The dancer flows.

An audience of apples bubbles beneath.
Several windfalls plop applause. Apples
gather like galaxies, like visitors for eclipse.

We are out of buckets to pick them up.
Hundreds still on the tree. Hundreds harvested.
Pickers have not arrived to help.

Media coverage of the eclipse is vivid.
Images of the entire sequence–front page.
Trump's hawkish Afghanistan stance–back pages.

His last night comments destroyed a great day hopes.
I did not listen. I focused on light after the eclipse.
Donald, duck–your quack hopefully short as a tweet.

May Trump's path of totality be brief. May our nation
and the world remain safe, increase our cosmic
consciousness, become one. May the Aquarian Age begin.

Commotion in the Canopy

Commotion in the canopy greeted me
as I went to contemplate post-eclipse
reality in the overcast backyard.

The hose moseys mid-way through the yard
separating picked windfall apples area
and unpicked apple-bobbers delight.

Bees hunker to the apple-bobbled side.
Bug-free, I sit on the barren side with
intermittent sun-shadow overlay.

Above a squirrel scampers apple-plum-
blue spruce to roof–tail waving,
making a flash appearance.

Birds fly canopy to canopy–not many
land on the empty plum and peach tree.
Apples and hazelnuts open for customers.

No LBJs or hummingbirds like yesterday.
Blue jays crack filberts on concrete wall and branches,
cast catches to the ground and fly away with them.

I watch the commotion, listen to squawks
and muted chimes. Much like anticipated
eclipse visitors not disrupting as much as expected.

They do not have a count of the crowd, but
mostly traffic did not jam, fires did not start.
Fascinated people acted with love not hate.

All creatures big and small, celestial objects
light or dark enacting roles in some cosmic plan.
Some players elicit fear and some delight.

Overcast

This late August, overcast morning,
the backyard looks bedraggled,
limping into autumn.

No roses, no gladiolas, no cherries,
no plums, no peaches-- only hazelnuts,
and apples plopping to hit the dust.

The peach tree is lopsided,
dropping barren branches, bent
like a cane. Not peachy this year.

Chilly, tepid breeze elicits
muted wind chimes, little
bird chatter or visits. No squirrels.

Apples bubble all around me.
Daily droppings overfill bucket
capacity and willing takers.

Beside me is a molded, concrete cherub,
reclining with hands behind head, sash
strategically placed to conceal gender.

Dirt makes it look rusted. Eyelids
closed, gifted cherub relaxes on the blue
round table oblivious to surroundings.

The rusted angel flying in the filbert tree,
I named Airlika. This cherub I'll call Bottom—
bottom on the yard and on its bottom.

The yard is too bent, too quiet, things
are falling, nothing is flying. Leafy-lace
shadows dimmed by clouds.

The backyard reflects my somber mood,
state of a troubled nation I had hoped
the solar eclipse would shift for brighter future.

The Apple Pickers

Tell what is in front of your nose. Gwendolyn Brooks

My friend Brigitte, a gardener poet,
helps pick two days of windfall apples
to make apple cider.

She has two large plastic bins,
she moves like a bulldozer
to clear the dappled lawn.

Apples caught in wall cracks, or
sprawled randomly across browning grass.
Stoop and plop, stoop and drop.

I watch from a chair and chat,
spot an apple in a notch
of the hazelnut tree–out of reach.

She is bendable and adept at the task,
filling bins with hundreds of apples–
two wheelbarrow loads to her car.

My husband will be so grateful for respite
from gathering buckets full of apples
almost daily with hundreds more to come.

He has lined up the buckets for visitors–
Scrabble players, writers, our Huddle–
Writing the Wrongs to Rights to bring home.

One friend needs them for her horses.
Others just to nibble the organic fruit,
create apple delights to their fancy.

Our daughter took wood from cherry tree's
demise. Hopefully family will pick up apples.
My husband does not want one to go to waste.

He digs out worms, slices scales, any defect
removed, diced and put on cereal, salad–
sometimes into apple sauce.

I do not pick or eat apples. An apple a day
probably would not keep the doctor away for me.
But my wish for the apple pickers–be well.

Lines

Driving home from exercise class
ten contrails crossed the sky-
two formed an X - diffusing.

When I went into the backyard for chi,
my husband is reel-mowing east and west
part of his S-N, E-W, then diagonal patterns.

He claims research found grass likes to be cut,
it energizes their growth and they are grateful
to him for mowing them down. Give him kudos.

He keeps a record of when and how he mowed.
Since it is summer and dry–this is a monthly mow.
He does not water grass, lets fall rains refresh.

He says the grass feels more virile cut–
What? Grass is male and likes vasectomies?
Nonsense. What about female grass?

One, I do not think grass has gender
Two, women would not want to be whacked.
Three, regardless I don't think grass likes cutting.

This line of thought is ludicrous, illogical.
When he hoe-claws crabgrass and lone dandelion,
he is trying to prevent re-seeding. I like dandelions.

He is more diligent against weeds in the front yard.
I enjoy seeing dandelions pop yellow, turn gray.
Since apples were picked yesterday, lawn less pimpled.

He still had to pick about a bucket before he could mow.
One stray apple met the blades and sliced. He moves on,
so did I. I went inside to avoid more slaughter.

If everything has energy, consciousness and is connected,
where are the boundaries? Should contrails spew on sky?
Should people decide how high grass should grow?

Why do we designate a plant as a weed? Prejudice?
In a chaotic world, how much are we to control or can?
Who gets to decide preference and dominance? Line up?

Here and Elsewhere

After the Art and Air Fair, we put our purchase
of two metal dragonflies on one spiral stalk
into a crack in the concrete chunk wall.

Two apple trees shaded them, so only shadow-breaks
would let their blue and copper glass eyes
and knife-blades, silver wings glisten in sun.

They both spun in breeze, but I wanted them to sparkle.
Later we moved them into a wooden bucket with sun-access
and brought a solo, straight-rod dragonfly to join them.

My husband said what I thought were bees
on the apples were wasps and they are getting
a little bit too friendly and buzzing me inside.

Yet with hurricane Harvey hitting the Texas coast,
Inconvenient Sequel showing fish swimming
on flooded streets in Miami, ice calving, drought--

all matter of climate changes and inept leadership,
our backyard is warm, breezy, quite quiet, cared for.
The movie haunts me as I sit drawing chi in socks.

A hummingbird to my left flutters facing me.
A black cat with white paws, meanders to sleep
on the wall and grass- then slinks through fence.

Apples drop and roll. Few birds, as few filberts left.
Images of global climate change whirl my thoughts,
but locally: impact of eclipse on environment minimal.

Oregon had no visitor-induced fires, few medical emergencies.
People mostly obeyed no campfire rules, picked up litter.
All the planning went smoothly. If only this were true elsewhere.

People planned food and fuel, avoided horrific traffic jams
but some delays. Everyone seemed well-behaved, neighborly,
connected to the cosmos on this small planet in a vast universe.

With the daily deluge of overwhelming bad news,
good news of good people trying to change things now,
here and elsewhere, lifts hope for a better future.

The dragonflies blink and wink light, twirl.
They brighten my mood as I go inside
to contemplate what's next?

Clearing

This late-August, mid-morning, my husband
clears the upper backyard of our fifth acre
between the upper and lower walls plateau.

He replaces a slat of rotted back fence
shared by two neighbors, ties a raspberry bush
with heavy string and nibbles berries delightfully.

I decide to sit and watch, try to chat
despite background sounds of a tree chipper
nearby, a plane and various bird squawks.

He pulled grape root from hard ground
and vines from plum and apple branches.
They were a seedy grape he did not like.

He whacked back white iris blades over-hanging
the higher, sidewalk chunk wall. Blackberries bushes,
English ivy removed. Both are too invasive.

He dug out many iris bulbs, pruned an ailing
azalea, clipped water sprouts under a filbert tree.
Birds devour our entire organic crop this year.

Our hazelnuts are doing well though state crops
are down about 18% due to blight. Oregon provides
99% of US crop and 5% of world supply.

He picked a five-gallon bucket full of apples.
Thwarted wasps. An un-identified sprig
sprawling through fence is unseen now.

Near the fence hidden in foliage, he found
we had a few red roses. A few, feeble, thirsty
gladiolas hang on. He yanked any dandelions.

A small windfall pear bodes well for more.
He finds a lost small clipper to add to his saw,
lopper, large clipper, two-sided hoe he uses.

He puts branches, sticks, foliage into a wheelbarrow,
tosses debris into piles for the recycling cart.
He carries tools to the garage for next time.

All this clearing is a distraction from grieving
the stunning, unexpected loss of a dear friend. I'm trying
to clear heavy remnants, revive memories of her light.

83

Renewal

The hose sprinkles the strawberry patch.
Perhaps some wind-wisps will moisten the glads.
The lawn remains un-watered in summer.

Last night we gave four buckets of apples
for a friend's horse and today—constellations
more. One pattern--like the Big Dipper.

Soothing mourning doves coo.
I barely don't overhear neighbors talking.
Wind-chimes rustle, but don't tink.

Too early for the full wasp brigade to bomb
the windfall apples? One wasp whizzes
by my head–drawn by arnica on my knees?

Smoke from Cascades' wildfires invades
a morning about to get really hot by afternoon.
A lazy haze covers the yard.

I grieve the loss of another close friend.
Lately several friends have moved away,
several friends have also died.

I am trying to compose an elegy for Jayne,
though it may be prose, as she was not
a fan of poetry. Now I'm lost in mind-fog.

Sun-sparkles on three metallic dragonflies
distract me-- a welcome thought-diversion
as I mull what can renew my spirits.

Meditating on Jayne

When we find someone who is brave, fun, intelligent and loving, we have to thank the universe. Maya Angelou

The rusty angel Airlika toots her horn
flying from the limb of the hazelnut tree
in noon-shadow with hazy, gauzy air.

A hacking cough from back neighbor,
a train whistle, tinkling wind-chimes,
leaf-rustling filbert-snatchers and cheeps.

Jayne told me to sit in this backyard at sunrise
to draw chi to heal my knees and aging ailments.
My observations became *Red Cape Capers*.

A fair-weather chi-catcher, I went inside
in bothersome weather and never really became
focused on meditation–especially at sunrise.

But this June after a few years lapse,
my massage therapist again sent me
to draw chi to energize my root chakra.

Ironically I resumed the practice about when
Jayne died and Airlika angel arrived from
another friend shortly after-- caring comfort.

Jayne came to town for a few years,
was assigned to Manzanita then Vancouver.
While she was here–I was part of her mission.

Jayne was a healer–hands on, essences and oils,
energy activation intuitive with close cosmic connections.
She introduced me to spiritual realms I never knew.

She claimed my knees were the worst she'd seen
in her world-wide practice. It was due to my not
wanting to be here, but I had a contract to fulfill.

She claimed my diabetes was due to grief
over the death of my son. During an activation
he came to give me energy from Aldebaran.

Miraculously she found funding to go to Tulum,
Mexico to be part of the 12-21-12 celebration.
Her insights and revelations blazed amazing.

Jayne took my Write Your Life Story class
and introduced mostly more conservative classmates
to Emmanuel and other non-mainstream writers.

Despite her dislike for poetry (and she knew
her teacher was a poet) her first story was a poem
to all our delight. She was quirky, funny, joyous.

Jayne was otherworldly. She recognized me as
a cosmic companion–originally from the Dal
universe, most recently playing in the Pleiades.

We apparently had lives as counselors
in many galaxies and many positions–
this lifetime as light-bringers to Earth.

Her enthusiastic, loving, healing spirit
opened new avenues to explore. I never
knew what Jayne was going to propose next.

When in town we would eat at a French restaurant
and her favorite sushi place. She would bring sushi
home to her daughter Morgan. The staff loved her.

Jayne gave me a fabric blonde angel
for my burgeoning angel collection, inscribed
in pink thread: Special Agent Linda V. Smith.

Jayne is my special agent angel.
Airlika will retain her sparkle for me
to recall and meditate upon.

Jayne probably would not like poetic lines,
so for her memorial I will write a prose
acrostic elegy in gratitude for her light.

A Moment of Tranquility

The dangerous air pollution
from wildfires in the state
has passed through–for now.

Under blue sky, I'm comfortable
before later hot temperatures--
breezes refreshing and calming.

An apple dangles and sways
from a slim limb. Two buckets
of windfalls picked up this morning.

The daily butterfly appears, but
few jays, few LBJs – no squirrels.
Shadows sprawl slowly. Gentle chimes.

Corvallis was polled as the safest
town and Houston the most dangerous
place in the nation.

Here I sit in safety, as hurricane
Harvey endangers Houston area
and moves into Louisiana.

The news shows unprecedented flooding,
threats of more dams and reservoirs
overflowing, levees breached.

A chemical plant might explode,
power gone to thousands, rescuers
bringing people to cavernous shelters.

Volunteers pitch in. Generous donations
of help. People working together,
stepping into other people's shoes.

Whenever there is a catastrophe, people
pull together temporarily, search for prevention,
fund renewal, try to rebuild lives.

In this already turbulent time for nation
and planet, compassion overloads.
Hope's threatened. We yearn for safety.

Just Chilling

Apples litter the light-dappled lawn.
Translucent leaves wiggle in breeze.
Shadows stretch across the entire yard,

The trees are bird-less as day fades,
except for a lone stellar jay in the blue spruce.
A scrub jay grubs ground at cherry tree's grave.

A few nut-crackers knock nuts against rock
and bark. Pesty wasps returned to nests?
Muted bird calls from other backyards.

An apple plops, distracts me from my
reveries of the cooperative Scrabble players
joyously scribbling tiles onto the witchy tablecloth.

I wore my purple Dare to be Outrageous tee:
Be playful enough to be noticed wherever you go!
It worked for several occasions today.

Our exercise class colluded to concoct outfits
to unnerve our fashion-coordinated teacher
who points out who falls short. We all did.

The eye-jarring event was to thank her
for teaching free all summer. We gave her
a subscription to Vanity Fair and ate cake.

I was underdressed and a tad inappropriate
for lunch out with Maureen Frank to thank her
for the stunning illustrations done for *Mirabilia*.

But sitting outside about 7 in cooling down heat,
I feel comfortable being colorful, unnoticed.
Just chilling out after a pleasurable day.

Getting Grounded

Reality is limited. Imagination is boundless. Favorite quote of a friend.

Leaves shadow-dance in the breeze
moving patterns across the grass,
to sound of wind-chimes.

Apples plop, punctuating thoughts.
No birds trigger the windfalls--
several bubble quite close to me.

It is mid-afternoon, much later
than sunrise, when Solara Jayne
told me to go barefoot to soak up chi.

After a chi hiatus, my massage therapist
Barbara told me to boot my root chakra
by connecting cosmic and earth chi.

Ironically, I returned to backyard backup
around the time of Solara Jayne's death
by another healer trying to ground me.

Barbara balances and clears chakras,
modifies my diet and massages muscles.
These healers help hitch me to Earth.

I've been called a "reluctant astronaut",
loosely attached to the planet I have been called
to serve as a light-bringer.

I'm like a balloon, a flight risk,
not knowing when I will burst, tethered to Earth
by my husband holding my string tightly.

As I explore 3D reality, endlessly curious
about the ground rules and my part at this time
in the grand oneness of ALL, I dream.

Multidimensional me is boundless.
My imagination is my celestial contact
while grounding this earthly experience.

As I contemplate, I can conjure fairies
swinging on apples. Metal dragonflies sway shade,
as a rusty angel under filbert limb toots her horn.

Transitions

Labor Day Weekend Sunday I wobble
to the backyard to witness the transition
to autumn amid residual smoke and heat.

Birds pilfered most of the filberts.
No fair-weather harvesters in sight.
Even wind-chimes still.

Five apples plopped since ground cleared
just hours before, but none while
I peruse backyard conditions.

One red rose peeks through bush.
Glads have given up.
Only apples to windfall into fall.

The Northwest endures forest fires,
three-digit heat, dangerous smoke.
My head feels stuffy, nose puffy.

Meanwhile hurricane Harvey
floods the Texas coast with fires,
destruction, polluted water and disease.

Congress will be coming back from vacation
and we will see how effectively D.C. handles
the crises and challenges this nation faces.

Around the world stories of suffering,
migration, warfare, climates changes--
remain present no matter what the season.

With my change in diet, frankincense
and arnica on knees, I feel more balanced
since solar eclipse. I sense I am healing.

I am in finishing stages for *Mirabilia*.
This poem is last chi poem for this book.
I am ready to start my next book.

Many changes occur on many fronts.
I scramble to keep up and filter--
gleaning light to soothe darkness.

Spirit

It does not matter how long
you are spending on the earth,
how much money you have gathered
or how much attention you have received.
It is the amount of positive vibration
in life that matters.

Amit Ray

Speculations

Perhaps if all systems are go
you can just let go
and go with the flow?

But if you're mentally ill
not cured by a pill
lost control of your free will...

it would be hard to connect
to higher self to perfect
when you sense a defect.

You may be in a situation,
even if you have intuition
you can't change destination.

So the on-going guru series
filled with uplifting theories,
might not answer your queries.

Dimmed and diminished minds
can't reach elusive light finds
of luckier, well-guided kinds.

We may all be starseeds
but have very different needs
from maybe diverse breeds?

Yet does the universe expect
all to shine or neglect
some with varying concept?

If we all are sparks of the divine,
somehow along the grape vine
some folks still stand in line.

We see such suffering and pain,
mistakes repeat again and again.
What learning do we gain?

I detest aspects of Earth's rules,
misguided ideas taught in mismanaged schools.
Can't there be some empathetic entity that overrules?

In the Flow

Relax. Find your flow, that's yours and yours alone, and ride the wave that is your life. Everybody has their own current and their own flow and your job is to figure out where is yours. Oprah Winfrey

Just a few ponderings flow by me--
Where does each flow originate?
Created before birth, energy implants
in the womb, seeking resonance
with energies in your existence location?

What entity or committee imparts
the individual's essence flow?
Does one's flow last for several incarnations
or dimensions in the multiverse?
How many waves does each soul ride?

Is our job to find our own flow
after we entered a lifetime
from a wavelength determined
with or without our consent
before each entered each consciousness?

Sometimes I think Cosmic Casting
sends out a call for sentient slots
for multiversal plots. Do actors audition?
Some parts are more desirable than others.
How do directors choose the best actor for a role?

Do actors get a chance to look at the scripts?
Can they select the parts they want to play
or assigned from previous performances?
Are some more gifted, get priority, a star?
Who writes scripts and selects actors?

In producing ALL there are infinite parts to cast.
Many stages, costumes, parts- leads and minor
characters, stagehands, musicians, ticket sellers
and takers, types of shows. Some ad libs?
Comedy or tragedy all have cosmic collaborators?

Between plays, movies, media productions
awaiting the next casting call, can we deliberate
how to get better roles? Caught in earthly karma?
Do we go off script in a good/evil tussle
or prefer a documentary for some cause?

Are plot points altered off-site
or at a destination? Can you refuse,
edit a script or re-write destiny?
If we arrive unscripted, do we make waves?
Drama, trauma, meditative choices?

Are angels our agents or managers?
Are we hard-wired for certain receptions?
Are we coded in DNA? Dealt limitations?
High tide or low tide, the surfer rides the wave
when you talk of an Earthling in current life?

How much of our consciousness is predetermined?
How much wiggle room? Cosmic help-line? How much adaptation?
How much do we act for ourselves? For others?
Ride the wave creatively, with purpose, joy
or swim through polluted seas?

Figuring out where my wave is-- my job?
Will I know if I have found it? Done well?
How many interactions with creatures
and environments will it take for my wave not to be
metaphorical or crash whitecaps on some shore?

Energy waves could waiver, resonate differently
collaborate cosmically in many configurations?
How I interpret my place in the cosmos and
this current lifetime– I must bear some responsibility.
A life without meaning, acting passively, not my choice.

Wherever my part in any flow, I hope
it flows lightly, nourishes, creates.
How much control I have, I do not know.
But as long as I'm conscious, I can try
to figure out my desired role in any reality.

A Winding Path

There is a winding path leading through a jungle of science and philosophy from the initial bland assumption that we people are physical objects obeying the laws of physics, to an understanding of our conscious minds. Daniel Dennett

Did we go from a soul-less to soulful world?
When and how did this happen?
Is consciousness's multi-layered computer
programs running on the hardware of the brain?

Science and philosophy have many theories.
Consciousness is a confounding concept.
Does it need bodies or operates formless
through many universes and dimensions?

How is consciousness attracted
to formulate an idea or form?
How does it communicate energy—
as a wave, invisible pattern or code?

Where does my consciousness originate?
What controls what I receive and perceive?
When the brain is damaged by plaque
or malfunction, did consciousness do it?

Is All consciousness and energy?
Just how does it all work, know where to go?
Fascinating, mind-boggling contemplation
for a minuscule, mini-byte, lost in the cosmic jungle.

An Un-blissful Truth

Remember you are just like all those Spiritual Teachers we see. You are just as divine and perfectly flawed. The difference is that you actually talk about it.
Marilyn Alauria

Spiritual teachers slant the truth for the New Age.
They tell you the techniques you can do
to live blissfully in the light and engage
on a enlighten path if you follow through.
      When things do not go right,
      eventually you'll find times of light.

They tell you the techniques you can do,
suggest they live in constant cosmic bliss.
Connect to the Universal Source and you
can also live divinely like this.
      Even if you get bumped from the path,
      reconnect for promise of better aftermath.

To live blissfully in the light and engage
while drawing closer to your truth,
you will trip and slip, write a new page,
become your own spiritual sleuth.
      Perhaps your truth is within
      and is the place you should begin.

On an enlightened path if you follow through
you could find spiritual guides and teachers,
ways to pray, meditate, connect to Source, pursue
a spiritual path, seek out-reachers
      who take your heart and hand,
      help you balance and understand.

When things do not go right
pick yourself up and know things can get better.
You are a learning, growing, bright
being composing your own life letter.
      Love yourself, tell your truth as you go
      find your bliss only you can know?

Eventually you'll find times of light
when things don't tend to darkle.
Stumbling off track can be set aright--
no one can continually sparkle.
      Try to carry on despite doubt.
      Who knows what bliss is all about?

Things Get Messy

Sometimes I'm the mess. Sometimes I'm the broom. On the hardest days I have to be both. Rudy Francisco

Sometimes I'm the mess–
messed up in mind and in my actions.
Sometimes I'm the broom of tidiness
sweeping from others' reactions.
> Hard days when I am both
> I lean toward light like a moth.

Messed up in my mind and in actions–
forgetful, fuzzy, careless, anxious,
I need to make some retractions,
try to rectify the angst and fuss.
> Unfortunately it takes time to clear
> and mend relationships I hold dear.

Sometimes I'm the broom of tidiness,
cleaning up dirt and debris.
A vacuum cleaner would be a plus
when setting things aright, neatly.
> But residues of hurt remain.
> Lots of confidence to regain.

Sweeping from other's reactions
requires I understand the situation.
Sometimes I misread difficult interactions
and need more tools than persuasion.
> Am I sweeping under the rug
> or just shrug–humbug?

Hard days when I am both
the problem and the solution,
when gleaning clarity seems mammoth,
it is a struggle to find resolution.
> When messing up it's my responsibility
> to restore order and release hostility.

I lean toward light like a moth
when life darkens and I fumble.
I must pick up a dust cloth
to wipe up when I stumble.
> Life gets messy, hard to heal.
> My techniques are far from ideal.

Left Behind

It is always harder to be left behind than to be the one to go. Brock Thoene

Sometimes I am glad to be left behind
    if the trip is too challenging I find
        and not going along is actually kind.

Sometimes I'm happy for the one leaving.
    Sometimes their absence is relieving
        or someone is moving forward after grieving.

Sometimes when it's my time to go
    I want those left behind to know
        it's hard because I loved them so.

Both Wings

Both wings are needed to soar. Sandra Bean

The oneness of humanity
is the animating principle of Baha'i.
Men and women are equal partners
if civilization's wings can fly.

The world's people have two wings--
need equally developed women and men.
Progress for women is incomplete.
Worldwide equality is uneven.

Certain cultures promote equality,
with laws and regulations
to see women get equal opportunity
to resources and education.

Humanity can't soar with weak wings.
Wings need strength, and ability to fly.
We can't clip and cripple so many wings,
nesting so many, we can't justify.

Seeking Truth

Hypostatize: to trust or regard (a concept, idea etc.) as a distinct substance or reality. Dictionary.com

Perhaps it is my inability to hypostatize
to commit to a truth or theory of anything.
I probe, research and hypothesize.
I've given up on a Theory of Everything.
> Can ancient wisdom and technology meld?
> What are the discoveries our ancestors held?

To commit to a truth or theory of anything
makes me feel boxed, unable to explore.
What does a consensual consensus bring?
Somehow I am always looking for more.
> I can't push the cloud of unknowing
> and find my ignorance is showing.

I probe, research and hypothesize.
Still understanding is out of reach.
I try various concepts, compromise,
but find much to learn before I teach.
> Certain basics I discover
> might be things to think over.

I've given up on a Theory of Everything--
a preoccupation of scientists.
With spirituality they are squabbling
over why All exists.
> I can't solve the mystery.
> No cosmic detective in me.

Can ancient wisdom and technology meld
to increase our understanding?
So many connections are being upheld.
The possibilities are outstanding.
> Ideas from our distant past
> are concepts we have found to last.

What are the discoveries our ancestors held
that remain timeless for our present day?
Beliefs about otherworldly contacts unquelled.
So many ooparts get in the way.
> The human brain and technology evolved.
> We don't comprehend all that's involved.

Lighter Realms

The lighter world of fairies, elves, gnomes,
otherworldly beings of lighter composition,
they lurk wherever imagination and curiosity roams.
I worry about people's imposition.
   Our 3D reality might impinge theirs.
   We might be harming them unaware.

Otherworldly beings of lighter composition
can be spotted by clear-seeing eyes.
Some witness nurturing, dancing disposition.
Some consider devas and spirits wise.
   Living on a parallel dimension from us
   might protect them from our fuss and muss.

They lurk wherever imagination and curiosity roams.
I want to believe their essence is real,
they have dance circles and mound homes.
I'm drawn to their surreal appeal.
   The possibilities are limitless and bright
   if we use our discretion and insight.

I worry about people's imposition
of our pollution nibbling their skin and wings.
our environmental and climate change position,
in this world, we share these things.
   If they are dimming, can't energize,
   what could we do to subsidize?

Our 3D reality might impinge theirs.
We are solidly grounded, messing up.
Do they think nobody cares?
How can we refill our shared cup?
   Do dimensional vibrations intersect?
   In what ways could we connect?

We might be harming them unaware
thinking we are the only sentient folk.
We waste water, clog up the air,
making all beings on earth choke.
   We can say they exist only in imagination,
   but we might share planet and destination.

Customer Service

Earth Planetary Planning Commission:

This is a request to review Earth's operations.
Surely an evolutionary update or cosmic jolt
is due, since we are messing up globally.
I am overwhelmed with its negativity.

The scuttlebutt is some Omni-Sparkler
energizes the cosmos by sending
soul-splinters of its essence to experience
vicariously the various experiments it sets in motion.

Perhaps things got a little overwhelming
for the Omni-sparkler and O-S delegated
procedures to a committee or energy-source
for each galaxy or trickle down to each planet.

In any case, whatever is puppeteer
for the puppets on this planet, the strings
are entangled and clear energy is muddled.
How can Earthlings perform with damaged strings?

Is the Earth plan to plunk, fleshy, fragile beings
into a dual 3D reality to see if the light side
can defeat the dark side? Do we really learn
from pain and violence? Who would choose that?

I'd like a lopsided toward light planet
with the darkness only shadows and night.
Earth is prone to upheavals and extinctions.
Aren't there less traumatic ways to change?

Why do we have to cry to unite people?
Can't we dance for joy for a blissful existence?
Why the challenges and obstacles? We could
create and appreciate faster with love, not fear.

The living conditions for billions on this planet
are appalling, the filth, inequities of resources,
sexist and racist agendas, degrading environment,
and the intimidation of violence. Waste of war.

Does it take a United Nations declaration
or will it be orchestrated by the Other Side
(If other-worldly beings want to bother)?
Perhaps we are trauma/drama entertainment?

I'd like to declare this experiment a failure
and request a change of approach by the guardians.
People are pawns suffering, so a long-distance
entity does not have to do so? Why anyone?

What is the purpose of sentience if not to better
cosmic conditions. Do we need all the blocks
to our creativity and enjoyment of this existence?
We're to be grateful to some divine source for this test?

I do not want to learn at anyone else's expense, or
by anyone's suffering. Can't we be nurturing and supportive,
innovative and elevating without hurt and impairment?
When will Earth have more sustainable stewards?

What is the benefit of living on Earth if you
only experience a limited life–aware of such
misery and unattainable abundance?
Could Earth become a vacation paradise instead?

We have had horrendously hard times in the past also.
We did not seem to learn from them–not even avoidance.
We still have war, waste, exploitation which
our technology accelerates–to our own extinction?

Whoever holds the strings to this ornery ort
in the multiverse, why not revise the plan?
Give Gaia's tenants another operational system
that glorifies the beautiful possibilities of Earth.

Love and light are great goals, but mostly illusions now.
Dreams and hopes remain inaccessible to most beings.
If I had confidence some essence sees a brighter change ahead,
I might carry my weary, heavy burden with less resentment.

Angelic beings from other dimensions, will you bring
a message of good will to your spirit-crushed, responsibilities?
Or are we caught in this chaotic, quagmire alone?
Or do we share this experimental fate with all other cosmic beings?

I doubt I'll get a response and will have to serve my life sentence.

Lai It On Me

What am I gleaning
of this life's meaning?
        Not much?

Mind-swept from cleaning
body demeaning
        and such?

Forces convening?
Maybe my screening?
        I'll clutch?

What angel leaning?
What knowledge preening?
        What crutch?

Sentience greening?
Who's intervening?
        Light touch?

The Path to Moksha

Hindus believe everyone ultimately wants to unite with the infinite–that which doesn't die or pass away. Union with Ultimate Reality of the Absolute is referred to as "moksha" or liberation. Karyn Chambers

Always interested in getting some enlightenment,
I read about many alternative points of view
explaining how I got into this earthly predicament.
Moksha unshackles death, birth and darkness too.
    Moksha seekers are single-minded and vigilant,
    rise above opposites, become an equality participant.

I read about many alternative points of view.
Am I a soul-splinter of some Omni-sparkler source?
To do yoga, meditate, self-inquire, find guru
is a Hindu path to their spiritual resource.
    Detach from the world. Search for the infinite.
    Obtain a calm mind, patience, deliverance is definite.

Explaining how I got into this earthly predicament
as a Hindu with burning faith and self-surrender,
for me is not the answer to my Gaia experiment.
I'm not an ego-less, emptied-mind, inward-turned contender.
    The knot between Self, pure consciousness resolves
    and with the physical body dissolves?

Moksha unshackles death, birth and darkness too.
If it allows me to explore, be multi-dimensional
maybe some life time, I'll be a Hindu.
I want life experiences to be intentional.
    If we see our own source and become that Self,
    and can it can happen in an instant- New-Self?

Moksha seekers are single-minded and vigilant
I splay my attention, not committing yet.
I am curious, well-intentioned and diligent.
Love freedom, compassion. What's best bet
    to find happiness, beauty, love?
    Depends on interpretation of above?

Rise above opposites, become an equality participant,
liberated from suffering, know truth and become one.
Many beliefs advocate similar goals-- it's significant
many light-bringers want positivity for everyone.
    Whether I become free, align or not,
    I'd like to solve humans' juggernaut.

The Path Ahead

With the choice of infinite paths we must intuit the way ignoring what fear may mock our progress. The path ahead will clear. The angels have promised.
Cindy Ruda

In these dark times of fear and violence
angels could have a hard time being heard.
Light-bringers need resilience.
I hope the angels keep their word.
> Do we have infinite paths and choice?
> Can we intuit what to give voice?

Angels could have a hard time being heard
amid the chaos, noise, destruction.
Some folks find angel concept absurd
and look elsewhere for instruction.
> However we get there, I hope the path clears
> and all might not be as bad as it appears.

Light-bringers need resilience
to be beacons on divergent paths.
Earthlings could shine their brilliance
to assure more hopeful aftermaths.
> In dark times we look for light
> when things are bad- set aright.

I hope the angels keep their word.
I wonder who they are telling this to
and when this promise to us occurred?
It would be helpful to have a clue.
> How do we intuit to clear the way
> so everyone can hear what angels say?

Do we have infinite paths and choice?
What is blocked or hidden?
It seems too early to rejoice
when access may be forbidden.
> I want to be hopeful for the best
> and up for any challenging test.

Can we intuit what to give voice?
Can we raise our vibes to be more intuitive
to connect with higher selves, check invoice?
Can we create lives less punitive?
> I've seen many angel numbers about.
> Angels, can you give me a shout?

Momentary Joy

Momentary joy punctuates a day
with exclamation points and interrobangs
while at other times fragments
into dashes and hyphens
brackets and parentheses
question marks and periods
commas, colons and semi-colons
ellipses, asterisks and slashes
during our life sentence.

To Become a Leader

If you want to become a pundit or guru
you select the message you want to say.
You tell other people what to do,
in a persuasive, engaging way.
> It helps to be a fund-raiser.
> You'll be a faster trailblazer.

You select the message you want to say,
hoping others will tow the line.
Examine why you want to sway?
For earthly gain or divine?
> People face divisiveness and polarity.
> Are you offering connection and solidarity?

You tell other people what to do.
How did you come to these conclusions?
Are your true intentions flowing through?
Is there a global need for your infusions?
> Why should people follow your word?
> Why should your outlook be heard?

In a persuasive, engaging way
we've had Hitler, Jesus, Buddha and Gandhi.
Troubling dynamics came into play.
I want kind actions, not mind candy.
> We need leaders against violence,
> ways to speak up, not silence.

It helps to be a fund-raiser
to get your points across.
To buy media attention, a clever-phraser
gets to be one's own boss.
> If leaders just did their mission
> for good, there would be less division.

You'll be a faster trailblazer
if you deliver love and service--
an equality-endorser, open-minded praiser.
Positive creativity could suffice
> to be part of solutions not the problem
> to bring sustainability not mayhem.

Overpowering Fear

People have always been afraid of what they do not understand, and they cannot trust the unknown, the strange and unfamiliar. Dolores Cannon

Most of the beliefs that divide
claim God's on their side,
stride with fearful pride, deride.

Fear seems a stumbling block,
many viewpoints can't unlock.
About time we took stock?

With extremists creating violence,
moderate voices tend to silence.
We need peaceful actions of resistance.

Can we cut the fear-tether
and begin to connect together?
Can we change emotional weather?

We are destroying life on the Earth.
Will we find another planetary berth?
How about clean up here for what it's worth?

We may move beyond the holographic
tied only by mind to Earth's geographic,
journeying among celestial traffic.

But while we are existing here,
can we try to set aside our fear?
We face dire times, it would appear.

Way-Showers

Wayshowers allow people to see their own paths so they can choose for themselves. Dolores Cannon

Fear is the root of all negative emotions.
Fear can prevent positive action.
Fear can warn to change demotions.
Fear requires healing reaction.
> Way-Showers provide growth for the soul.
> Way-Showers heal to make us whole.

Fear can prevent positive action.
We need to look within for the source,
re-balance an interaction
touch a vibrational resource.
> Find the surface and then root fear.
> Just what are we dealing with here?

Fear can warn to change demotions
to get us back on a better track.
Way-Showers with healing motions
can heal us where we lack.
> Touch gets information to assist.
> Fear and emotions can resist.

Fear requires healing action.
Way-showers can touch the third eye,
with clairsentience sense reaction,
get to healing ways to try.
> People can heal themselves then.
> A way-shower can sense when.

Way-Showers provide growth for the soul.
They work with conscious, so subconscious fears
can be brought to the surface and determine role
by asking questions, until realization appears.
> When way-showers touch they know
> by sensing and re-balancing energy flow.

Way-Showers heal to make us whole.
Many healers and many methods to explore.
Go forward. Don't hold onto the past. Roll
past fear present or past, once more:
> Left side ills dwell from past-right side present.
> Extremities are afraid to move on. Regain consent.

Self-Help

We live in an age of excitability, agitation and venting, thanks in part to our unprecedented leisure time and astounding technology. Yet we also want happiness, serenity and meaning which is why so many of us keep heading to the self-help section of the bookstore. Massimo Pigliucci

Some seek guidance from religion, New Age thought,
others search from ancient wisdom and an eclectic perspective.
Some explore widely and come up with naught.
others are reflective or play detective.
> What techniques help us navigate existence?
> Why are we feeling such insistence?

Others search from ancient wisdom and an eclectic perspective
what they do not find in the current mainstream.
Lots of choices so we can be selective.
What approach lets us reach our destiny's dream?
> Suppress suffering like a stoic?
> Act out and be heroic?

Some explore widely and come up with naught.
Nothing resonates so they can commit.
They just can't buy what is being taught.
There is always something they want to omit.
> We adjust responses to what's happening now.
> Endure what has to be endured somehow.

Others are reflective or play detective,
discover what is within their power,
contemplate the broader picture yet introspective,
think ahead about challenges beyond next hour.
> Be mindful of the here and now, be present.
> Set intention for an authentic precedent.

What techniques help us navigate experience?
Our free will supposedly lets us choose.
How will we use this lifetime's sentience?
Weigh what we gain or lose?
> I should not presume to give voice
> to interfere with another's choice.

Why are we feeling such insistence?
Some say we are feeling a global awakening?
We're raising vibration, heart energy, intelligence
to be part of a galactic undertaking.
> To be part of something on such a scale,
> I'll need self-help from beyond the veil.

111

The Test

It wouldn't be a test if you knew the answers. Dolores Cannon

Supposedly we are in the Earth School,
to pass tests for our spiritual growth or progress
in whatever areas we put into our Life Chart
before we entered this Earthbound incarnation.

But what kind of test are we taking
when we forget the questions at birth
and muddle through our lives being tested
when we don't know the goals or answers?

It would be helpful if we knew for what purpose
the questions are on the test we want to pass.
How much karma and suffering could be by-passed
if we had a clear agenda upon entry?

Why continually re-inventing the wheel,
re-starting after extinctions from scratch,
when supposedly the Akashic records
could be accessed for guidance?

If we have angels and guides to support us,
but they can't interfere unless asked
because we have free will, are they bored
or hyper-ventilating clouds into rain?

Supposedly we have a higher self
to which some people claim to have access,
Cosmic consciousness and connection
are these on the Earthling test?

If each life has meaning and a destiny,
why can't we remember it? We struggle
and hope we made the right choices
on multiple choice tests.

Do we each have a time-line before
we exit, graduate or perhaps held back?
As scientists contemplate a multiverse and
multi-dimensions–if I flunk out I'd have options?

The Dalai Lama Says

Once people adopt a religion, they should practice it sincerely. Truly believing in God, Buddha, Allah or Shiva should inspire one to be an honest human being. Some people claim to have faith in their religion, but act counter to its ethical injunctions. They pray for the success of their dishonest and corrupt actions, asking God or Buddha for help in covering up their wrongdoings. There is no point in such people describing themselves as religious.
The 14th Dalai Lama Tenzin Gyatso, spiritual leader in Tibet.

The Dalai Lama says the world faces a crisis due to lack of respect for spiritual principles and ethical values.
People need to develop convictions, find ethical principles to select not forced by society, science, or legislative point of view.

The Dalai Lama says many governments lack self discipline and self-restraint. Also citizens, CEO, lawmakers and teachers need to create a society based on inner cultivation of virtues that do not taint progress. Secularism, inclusiveness and diversity a priority?

The Dalai Lama says religion faces challenges from science, communism and consumerism. Tenets and beliefs require reason. Some people don't rely on sacred texts and are out of compliance. Perhaps other elements impinge and are considered treason?

The Dalai Lama says phenomena like rebirth and existence of the mind are beyond the scope of scientific investigation.
There is no proof they do not exist. They might find open minds, beneficial discussions improve the situation.

The Dalai Lama says faith traditions favor inner satisfaction and peace, not happiness through external objects.
Kindness, generosity, honesty are part of religious faction which instant gratification, consumerism often rejects.

The Dalai Lama says some of his teachings may be in harmony with your values on society, science and consumerism – or not.
Continue to investigate and reflect for your own discovery.
Base conclusions on reason not tradition, blind faith, peer pressure plot.

The Dalai Lama ponders some of the anger, suffering and violence people deal with in supposedly modern civilization.
Some of my nagging doubts, he does not totally silence.
I've still some slanted biases and asking "why" questions.

113

Spiritual Education

The primary, the most urgent requirement is the promotion of education. It is inconceivable that any nation should achieve prosperity unless this paramount, this fundamental concern is carried forward. Baha'i Sacred Writings

From the Baha'i perspective for humanity to progress,
we need an all-out effort to transform minds and hearts
to see as world citizens our common destiny and oneness.
We are interconnected, need to collaborate, do our parts.
     Can we free ourselves of social disease "isms"?
     Conditions that divide like racism, sexism, classism?

We need an all-out effort to transform minds and hearts.
Baha'i's spiritual education is a process of helping oneself
and others discover their true self. Find our counterparts.
Educational institutions created to know thyself.
     Gender equality is an emphasis in Baha'i writing.
     Past discrimination they are a-righting.

To see as world citizens our common destiny and oneness,
equality is a cornerstone of a stable and just society.
Educating women will ensure our progress is simultaneous.
We can work together to reduce global anxiety.
     Education of girls takes precedence over boys
     if family can only educate one—girl enjoys.

We are interconnected, need to collaborate, do our parts.
The social and economic advancement of women is a solution?
Baha'i's were pioneers creating educational starts.
But higher education rights hindered without resolution.
     A quasi-religious apartheid in business also exists.
     Still the Baha'i persists and resists.

Can we free ourselves of social disease "isms"?
Baha'i provide educational platforms on-line.
If they can't attend universities which imprisons
they find other ways to teach, keep ideas in line
     to develop human heart and a mature mind.
     Someday we're one family we could find.

Conditions that divide like racism, sexism, classism
Baha'i confront with a spiritual education.
Can we resolve every schism?
Despite one's religion or not can we make a transformation?
     We know people need to make a change,
     try harder for a sustainable exchange.

Conversing with Dr. Ravi Zacharius

Many times as Christian theists, we find ourselves on the defensive against
critiques and questions of atheists. Sometimes, in the midst of arguments and
proofs, we miss the importance of conversation. These questions, then, are
meant to be part of a conversation. They are not, in and of themselves,
arguments or "proofs of God." They are commonly asked existential or
experiential questions that both atheists and theists alike can ponder.
Ravi Zacharius. "Questions on the existence of God"

Agnostics and practitioners of many spiritual traditions
also ask these "big questions" and make own suggestions.
I tend to be of the unaffiliated persuasion.

1. **If there is no God, "The big questions" remain unanswered**, Ravi says.
   Why is there something rather than nothing?
   Why is there consciousness, intelligent life on this planet?
   Is there any meaning to this life?
   Does human history lead anywhere or is it all in vain since
      death is merely the end?
   How do you come to understand good and evil, right and wrong
      without a transcendent signifier?
   Whose opinion does one trust in determining what is good or bad,
      right or wrong?
   If you are content within atheism, what circumstances would
      serve to make you open to other answers?

Believers and non-believers answer these questions based on their choice.
Not just Christians guide people's decisions, support their voice.
The freedom to seek, find own answers, makes me rejoice.

2. **If we reject the existence of God, we are left with a crisis of meaning.**
   In the absence of God there is no transcendent meaning
      beyond one's own self-interest, pleasures or tastes.
   Without God, there is a crisis of meaning, and (atheist) thinkers
      show us a world of just stuff, thrown into space and time
      going nowhere, meaning nothing.

This a slanted, judgmental point of view-- not one of all.
Christians have not the best record and only protocol.
I prefer thinkers open, ready for a speculative free-for-all.

3. When people have embraced atheism, the historical results can be horrific.
Ravi talks about Stalin, Mao, Pol Pot who saw religion as "a problem
to eradicate" and called them regimes with implications of atheism.
Socio-political ideologies could very well be the outworking of a particular
set of beliefs that posited the ideal state as an atheistic one.

What about the Crusades, Inquisitions, ISIS, endless God-fearing fights
over religion to impose one's beliefs on another, slavery, indigenous rights,
slaughters of populations who disagree with your faith, increasing plights?

4. If there is no God, the problems of evil and suffering are in no way solved.
Ravi asks where is the hope for redemption, or meaning
for those who suffer?
Without God there is no hope for ultimate justice, or suffering
being meaningful, transcendent, redemptive or redeemable.
Is there a God to reach out to for strength, transcendent
meaning or comfort?
Why would we seek the alleviation of suffering without objective
morality grounded in a God of justice?

Many traditions and thinkers have alternative solutions.
Many Christians have hypocritical resolutions.
After much study I do not believe Christian conclusions.

5. If there is no God, we lose the very standard by which we critique
religions and religious people.
Whose opinion matters most?
Whose tastes of preferences will be honored?
Who are we to give them meaning anyway?
Where do standards come from?
Human cultures have legally or socially disapproved of everything
from believing in God, world revolves around sun, slavery,
interracial marriage, polygamy to monogamy.
Human taste, opinion law and culture are hardly dependable
arbiters or truth.

Christianity was involved in suppression of science, decided
who to love, punished those who opposed, derided
other interpretations of truth. This quest is lop-sided.

6. If there is no God, we don't make sense.
How do we explain longing and desires for the transcendent?
How do we explain human questions for meaning and purpose?
Why do I feel unfulfilled or empty?
Why do we hunger for the spiritual?
How do we explain these longings if nothing can exist
beyond the material world?

I believe we are stardust, starseed beings part of ALL,
connected to cosmic consciousness, multidimensional,
spirits who came to Earth, responding to our call.

We come to learn and grow in Earth School,
we search for meaning, decide which ideas rule.
We are inhabitants of a larger cosmic pool.

Perhaps we come to be kind, bring love and service,
share our creative gifts non-violently, not sacrifice.
Not being considered Christian for me will suffice.

I don't place a spiritual label on my conclusions
as I dwell in surroundings some call illusions.
I resist hierarchical, religious institutions.

A Prime Creator, I refer to as the Omni-Sparkler
set many experiments into motion- a light-sparker.
Many beings enlight to prevent things getting darker.

Ravi and I will have to agree to disagree.
His interpretations don't resonate with me.
I want to remain open, responsible and free.

Interdependence

If we can think for ourselves, if we can be aware of our states of mind and heart, we can exercise an independence of spirit. For me this includes an appreciation both for the lives of those who are like me and not like me. It's harder to make assumptions and judgments. Abby Terris

At a Zen Interdependence Retreat
they refrained from speaking.
In silence less distracted, more complete,
to be in moment they are seeking
     own responsibility for the word.
     Modern life bombards us, is heard.

They refrain from speaking
review thoughts, intentions, actions.
Silence sensitizes, awareness peaking.
Cultivate kindness in interactions.
     Being more sensitive to words is seeing manipulation
     of story of experiences and increases your emancipation.

In silence less distracted, more complete,
remain aware of ourselves and think about
fixed narratives spun around us replete
with anxiety, worst in us and stirring doubt.
     So much media and political activity,
     we are in constant excitement and reactivity.

To be in the moment they are seeking
self-calming, and independence.
Through reflection they are ceking
how to respond, listen for interdependence.
     Are we Divided States of Fear,
     losing values we hold dear?

Own responsibility for the word--
no careless speech, unexamined assumptions,
reject fear and the absurd.
make fewer judgments and presumptions.
     Be aware of the state of your mind and heart,
     the divisive ideas that keep us apart.

Modern life bombards us, is heard
loudly to divide us, when we share existence.
United we stand. Divided we fall. Gird.
We can thrive with determined resistance.
     Be part of interdependence.
     Remember your independence.

The Power of Mindset

Napoleon Hill talked about the power of mindset. I don't know about you, but that was an area where I'd do great for a while; and then I'd fall down the darn rabbit hole over a random comment by someone else. I understood how important mindset is, but I couldn't keep it. Marilyn Alauria

My dictionary did not define mindset*,
but Hill suggests we need a mastermind group--
a support group to hold one's vision
and direct one back to it.

This mastermind group is a place
to explore ideas, get feedback and advice
to help you make wise decisions
while avoiding costly mistakes.

The group lovingly calls you out
when you fall off the path, shares
in your success and supports
you on your journey.

Sounds a lot like a writer's critique group,
a spiritual direction gathering,
an ego-boosting, judgmental support
group to offer unsolicited advice.

Who would be guiding your vision
you are creating from within?
Random comments that do not resonate
can't undermine your authenticity.

Like Alice, a trip down a rabbit hole
might open new worlds to explore.
My surreal, cosmic mindset needs
some grounding now and then.

Like anyone, I am discerning
about supporters and surroundings.
I rely on my inner insights and otherworldly
guides in my multidimensional quests.

* *The established set of attitudes held by someone.*
The mental attitude that determines how you will interpret and respond to situations. Dictionary.com

Flow

Flow is even not about when things are easy and effortless, although those are characteristics of Flow. That's because Flow is not about being led by ego/mind/ personality. Instead, its about letting the Universe lead. Sara Wiseman

Flow is being aligned with the Universe
in creative and spiritual activities.
We are not to force momentum–
just go with the flow.

Flow is about allowing ourselves
to follow signs and synchronicities in complete trust
as our way of being. Get out of our way and let
the Universe inform us and guide us.

We should heed our still, small voice, fight ego,
enter state of humility, let go of mis-beliefs,
societal illusions and move to state of wonder and awe.
Surrender to Divine guidance and live from understanding.

Well, I am not even sure I want to be in the Flow.
I accept we might be soul-slivers of ALL and have a mission
to contribute to the betterment of this world–or perhaps
not–be a foil, play a role for some other purpose.

For me creativity is more important than knowledge.
Many concepts are beyond my understanding.
I accept earthly life may be a holographic illusion
and I might be part of a computer program, begrudgingly.

Perhaps Universal Law is not to my liking
and different planets, dimensions, galaxies
have agendas that are repellant to my current beliefs.
If I play many roles and many places–just flow?

I have been told I came here reluctantly–
kicking and screaming until my "calling"
made me concede to come when I was perfectly
content living happily elsewhere.

I am supposed to accept the Universe can boss
me around, limit choice, lure me by signs,
tweak my codes into compliance, as I struggle
dealing with a troublesome existence.

Alas, there are probably multiverses with different
expectations. So I must adjust to new requirements
and another cosmic expectation, following Flow
or whatever guidance system put in place.

The Universe could be in upheaval, changing guard,
in a negative place, taken over by dark forces.
Am I to just flow with this situation hoping
for sentience and consciousness elsewhere?

If I am not in a Universe of light, love, kindness
working toward enlightenment, I am not interested.
Violence, hate, negativity–tired of suffering.
I'm protesting Flow that results in this type of existence.

How many lifetimes and experiments does it take
to create a Universe worth dedicating one's life for?
Space/time is a difficult concept, as is all happening Now.
Maybe that is why Flow has a way to go,

I live in a state of wonder and awe, insatiably curious.
I resist dark forces, injustice and hurt. Why is never
answered, quests do not resolve conflict but stir
new questions as to what to believe.

I am excited by new discoveries which are just
the latest understanding in flux and change.
I cling to beauty, the light beings enhancing hope
there is something, somewhere perfecting Flow.

Cycles

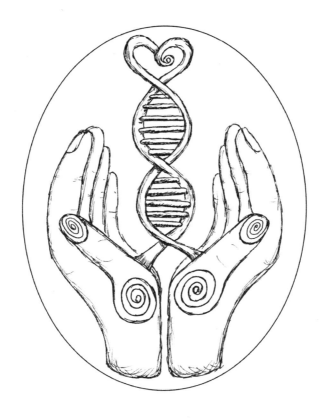

*Life is a repeated cycle
of getting lost and then
finding yourself again.
There are many smaller cycles
within that cycle where you get lost
to a smaller degree and then
remember yourself again.
Sometimes you do it on purpose,
consciously or unconsciously.
Every time you get lost
it is so that you can learn
or experience from a different perspective.*

Jay Woodman

She Who Cycles

We celebrate the distinction to unlearn the trance of equating Maidenhood with
reproduction and sexuality, focusing instead on sacred desire.   Kim Duckett

In May some traditions honor the patterns
replicating the seasons,
the waxing and waning of the moon,
the ebb and flow of ocean,
menarche in the bodies of women.
Women of all ages embrace their inner youth.

Women go on monthly vision quests
to look inward on sacred desire,
listening, not about reproduction
but sharing about the creation of the universe.
People ask women to remember magic.
From ancient times menstruation was considered
central to developing human civilization.

Women respond to both sunlight and moonlight
through pineal gland, hormones- the seat of the soul,
hormones dance and flow with forces of nature.
Cycling renews mental and physical health,
takes us inward and outward
to release what no longer serves us.

Desire is the Outward call
of our internal guidance system.
Menarche is the Inward call,
where we seek wisdom,
bring desires to fruition,
natural and personal cycles are one.

During this season, journey or quest
to learn new skills, practice balance
of self-care and care-giving,
inspiration from our gut to find
the genius only you can manifest,
ask Maens or Maidens in your life
and within yourself what you really desire.

Middlescence

The middle-age period of life, especially when considered a difficult time of self doubt and readjustment. Dictionary.com

How long do we stay in middlescence?
At what age do we enter and then exit?
We've an inkling of the length of adolescence.
When we're in top form and our body fit.
We steadily decline until we end it?

So what makes sense?
Mind and body age together?
How much are we in touch with soul's essence?
What check list determines whether
there's evidence?

Aging varies with the individual.
Sometimes the mind stays too long in pubescence?
Does it matter since death's eventual?
Do we await for onset of senescence?
How long do we stay in middlescence?

The Medicine Wheel

Great-Grandfather gave Native Americans spiritual guidance to pray, focus and grow spiritually through the Four Great Forces of the Medicine Wheel. We focus on these Four Great Powers for directions in all aspects of our world. Donna Vaillantcourt. In Apache Nina Osa or "little girl bear"

Her world tradition consists of birth, life, love,
growing, learning, challenge, change and death
spiritually guided by Great-Grandfather through
the Four Great Powers or Directions of the Medicine Wheel.

East brings eagle and illumination of the sun
for spiritual and intellectual enlightenment.
The color is golden for the sun giving our bodies
life, warmth, healing rays and mind stimulation.

South is for innocence and trust, examining nature
of our hearts as to who we truly are and find where
fear originates. The colors are brown and green
for Mother Earth, her grasses and many medicinal plants.

West is black for the sun leaves us in darkness.
The "Looks Within Place" to be introspective,
to examine your mind and heart for what is true.
Deal with questions to become whole.

North is to find wisdom and endurance.
The color is white for snow and ice.
Medicine animals wolf and buffalo can survive
in harsh, brutal conditions. Learn to endure hardships.

The black bear, medicine animal of the West,
hibernates to heal and renew. People can look within
to contemplate problems, emerge with East's illumination
see truth, gather wisdom and endurance from the North.

To survive and thrive, push away fear and pride
for Southern humility, trust and innocence.
Walk a mile in another's moccasins before judging,
overlook others faults while overcoming yours.

Lovely images of directional and seasonal cycles.
Whatever tradition guides you to look within
to know yourself and to connect to higher powers,
can better the world and all its creations.

Possible Realities

What choices do we have for reality?
 3D duality physical manifestation
on a gasping Gaia part of some experiment,
 escapes to drug-induced delusions,
processing problems causing mental illness,
 creating fantasy and sci fi possibilities,
tv, movie, smart phone screens, A.I. games,
 virtual reality, Second Life, avatars,
advances in A.I. so someday hybrids, cyborgs, robots,
 digital simulations like Metaverse 1.0
where you still keep a bio-body,
 or Metaverse 2.0 where you dump
digital consciousness into the Cloud
 and leave a physical body into a new species?

Are we already a simulation--
 a holographic projection
from some more advanced alien species?
 Is it all about how energy manifests here
or remains in another dimension?
 Free will and non-interference theories
so far have left this semi-consensual reality
 a divisive, violent, polluted mess.
Anywhere is a clean up crew present
 and creating a more peaceful, beautiful life?

As more options open up and people
 get a chance to leave pain and death behind,
they have no guarantee the new life experience
 doesn't get hacked and unplugged
by the negative forces we deal with now.

If we are all stardust, cosmic travelers
 experiencing for some not-really-clear reason,
no matter where we are, we are part of some network,
 caught in some web, sentient for an unknown purpose.
Some believe ancient knowledge will be found
 to explain what is going on. Others insist we will
increase our vibration to 5D and create a New Earth.
 Forces of love and light might someday intervene
to blow dark suffering away. Well, we can speculate
 divine or cosmic agendas, but so far I don't know
if my preferred reality will ever exist. I can dream,
 but I have to live with what I can detect.

Beyond Bones and Brains

...Your existence is a miracle
But don't force a smile
Instead, honor your humanity
Speak in sentences of bouquets and thorns... Kim Adonna

These miraculous bones and brains
contemplate planes less physical
to see what the cosmos explains
in sciences and the metaphysical.
      Speaking my sentences to the page
      I can express and re-engage.

Contemplate planes less physical–
is my present quest and fascination.
Prescience and the whimsical
prepare me for my ultimate destination.
      My body senses help me cope,
      but I want to open the envelope.

To see what the cosmos explains
and how it impacts my consciousness here
would help me navigate many terrains
until my limited body won't interfere.
      I think to travel light
      would be pure delight.

In sciences and the metaphysical
I try to find meanings for our existence.
So far answers leave me quizzical.
I sense my deep resistance.
      Operating brain and bone
      leaves me feeling lost and alone.

Speaking my sentences to the page
gives expression to my pondering.
I manifest thought to image,
reveal my spiraling wondering,
      about being multidimensional,
      exploring what's intentional.

I can express and re-engage
with the experiences as this being.
What discoveries can I stage
for the insights I'm seeing?
      Dwelling in and out of form,
      for me is becoming the norm.

Palimpsest

What's left is palimpsest—one memory bleeding into another, over-writing it.
What knowledge haunts each body, what history, what phantom ache.
                    Natasha Tretheway

When you think of what's encoded in our DNA,
brain chemistry network coding our thoughts,
add multidimensionality and multiple lifetimes--,
are we computer chips for the Akashic records' cloud?

Some perceive us as a thread in a tapestry--
a multiversal weaving of consciousness,
part of ALL, creation of an Omni-Sparkler
learning through soul-splinters of the divine?

Are we layers within ourselves
adding to the fabric of space?
Memories fading, re-writing over time?
Unaware of the experiences and consciousness within?

What phantom aches prod our reincarnations?
What knowledge haunts what we have hidden?
The complexity is mind and heart-boggling.
Our equipment does not seem up to the task.

If our life chart is erased before birth,
all our intentions have to be re-discovered.
Not the most efficient process, it would appear.
Just what is the ultimate goal?

Are we a palimpsest in body or not embodied?
Does our over-soul lug all our luggage for eternity?
Can we drop off some baggage in Akashic storage?
Energy and matter interact in mysterious ways.

I gave up the notion I can ever know it all
as long as I'm in this lower frequency, dense body.
This leaves something to look forward to when I'm lighter.
Some life excursion might contain more enlightenment.

My palimpsest could be erased or over-written
as long as my soul-sliver is sentient. If I'm null-and-voided,
I would not have any idea I ever existed. But then--
I never did know all of what happened to all my many-selves.

Remember It's Only a Story

For Maureen Frank

My collaborator for designing my books
is also intuitive. We sat down for a reading.
Both of our higher selves went on a journey.

Maureen described a cartoon-ish Dutch
boy (me) and girl (her) climbing an orange hill
over picket fence to a portal in an opalescent dome.

As an Aries, with adventurous energy,
I am hurrying her through a tunnel
to a surreal place called Storybook Land.

Each of us creates a story as a living,
breathing entity and we are in control
at all times. It's only an illusion.

* Pick a story.
* Live the story
* See it to its ending.

Through meditation I can use
this dimensional portal. While sleeping
I am an active dimensional traveler.

Apparently my wild dreams
are part of my traversing the cosmos
as consciousness through dimensions.

Currently, I am "house-hunting" for my next life's
destination. Sometimes I prefer a starship
rather than moving faster by consciousness.

At each stop I pick up flowers- symbols
of thoughts I can use in my poems.
Spiral Hands might be my last book.

Angel numbers are codes for my higher self.
I could relax and try to enjoy my unfolding story.
My celestial son Kip stopped by for a hi-flash.

My frequency is rising. I'm to increase
visualization and open up all my senses
to energize my story, breathe my butterfly's flight.

Maureen drew a watercolor painting
with her notes on the back for me
to re-envision our trip as well as other tips.

The sky is deep navy with sparkling stars,
constellations above white-tipped waves
of light-blue river leading into purplish portal entrance.

Orange fields (creativity color) with spiral
dots, the rainbow dome blending blue, rose,
green and yellow. Maroon entry fades to yellow.

A butterfly hovers over the life-river
leading to the portal to enter other dimensions.
The story-image dwells over my computer

The Energy Sieve

In the huge stadium for Oregon State University graduation,
I watch from the club level-- top tier-- the rows and rows
of chairs awaiting thousands of graduates as they parade
onto the field following bagpipes. Hoods, black gowns,
decorated mortar boards, color slashes of sashes and cords
draping their shoulders, tassels jouncing from their heads.

Cell phones communicate with thousands more
family and friends in the stands–cheering and waving.
Celebratory music played way before the parade.
Each graduate whatever level of degree gets
their own diploma– no mailing later. They line up and sit
precisely-- so no mess ups. Eight port-a-potties at edge.

It is the largest graduating class ever- 6,807
getting 7,097 degrees, Youngest 19. Oldest 74.
From all 50 states, 68 countries. The 148th graduating class
joins 243,081 previous OSU Beaver graduates.
The speaker Turkish billionaire 1967 grad Husnu Ozyegin.
Open seating for estimated 23,000. 4000 grads marched.

Closeups provided by jumbotron. Blasted canned music.
Mighty mics boomed the speeches. All the vibes. All the cheers.
I could just feel the energy pass through me. Think
of all the particles, sound waves drifting about in gentle breeze!
All the breathing. All the high emotions. All the smart phones.
Lots of love, pride and joy wafts through my skin, rushes to my core.

Waverly Duck

The duck triggers memories people have, and it represents membership in the
community...It reinforces how people integrated in the community.
Waverly Duck, associate professor of sociology at the University of Pittsburgh

Waverly Duck is a very dapper duck
artistically refurbished and returned
to Waverly Lake beside Waverly Road.

Waverly is a 500 pound spray-foam replica
of a wooden duck– a gigantic decoy
returned to water after rehabilitation.

Withdrawn from the pond in 2007
in derelict condition, ten years later
it was ready to refloat.

Green and yellow, University of Oregon colors--
the duck is as colorful as the volunteer-created animals
for the carousel, also in Albany opening soon.

Waverly and the carousel are community efforts
to brighten their town. Duck calls greeted Waverly's return.
The crowd cheered as the duck bobbed off the trailer.

A motor boat pulled the duck to mooring
in the center of the lake. The beloved duck
is ready for tourist appreciation.

Two local high schools captured the old duck
and hauled it to their school's parking lot
and courtyard for a prank. Will this replica remain?

Decades ago my daughter and I would greet
the original duck on our way to the freeway
en route to a year and a half in a Portland school.

Each morning no matter the weather we would
look for the duck as we began our journey. Then
the duck would usher our path back home.

I hope to see the new Waverly soon.
My husband and I plan a trip to Portland
to visit a friend and attend two poetry readings.

I must e-mail my daughter in Salem about the duck
so when she visits, she can be sure to take the route
beside the fondly-remembered, chuckle-inducing duck.

Sun-lit Bugs

Sun-sparkled bugs flit
        outside the window
on a warm, blue-sky May day
        darting and dashing
in the alley between
        a tall, sun-lit limbed evergreen
with some rusty under-branches
        and our house with a metal bird
dangling from the roof line.

The sun highlights a web-thread
        dangling from the roof,
but the bugs dodge it to fly freely,
        to other landings.
I hope the bugs stay outside
        to sunbathe.
I watch as the light shifts west,
        as shade, fades them out of sight.

Quintillas for Ants

An ant crawled on the bathroom floor
in a solitary parade
just big enough to not ignore
a black ort, small dot masquerade?
Usher ant gently out the door?

Slowly the ant scout sought its routes.
Naked, I watched its progress.
Stepped in shower. Did ant regress?
Must have escaped somewhere I guess.
Are other ant troops in cahoots?

Bigger ants, I don't hesitate
to squish, smash, stomp, stop in its tracks.
Destinations necessitate
taking action, participate.
I'd prefer to avoid attacks.

When I saw tiny, lonely ant,
another earthly habitant
who am I do douse its dreams
by my reacting with extremes?
Mission might be significant.

Why should I become so militant?
Who appointed me lieutenant?
So why am I so arrogant?
Why should I take life from an ant
because a minor irritant?

Cloud Creatures

I watch
cloud animals
nipped by darkened, brisk winds,
blown apart to re-group elsewhere,
vanish.

strawberry moon
faraway blush
in summerish sky.

The Eclipse Rides Through Corvallis
With the dawning of this eclipse. Maybe we can pay more attention, maybe we can respect our planet and ecosystem more. Maureen Frank

"The Eclipse Rides Through Corvallis"
is a street mural to celebrate bicycling
and the August 21st solar eclipse.

At Northwest 11th and Taylor 30 volunteers
painted a beautiful massive mural designed
by Maureen Frank–The Mandala Lady.

My husband and I drove over the mural
intersection from all four directions
to enjoy this collaborative community effort.

The mural is fifty feet in diameter.
Cutouts of design elements helped
volunteer painters be consistent.

A neighborhood association obtained the funds
from a $1000 neighborhood empowerment grant,
supported by a bicycle collective headquartered nearby.

Volunteers have agreed to an annual retouch party,
re-paint wheel-worn spots, refresh rain washes,
leaf-splats, muddy feet pedestrian peekers, sun-fade?

Open Streets project–a bike and pedestrian
festival held the day before the eclipse
hopes many more neighborhoods join in.

Murals on walls, murals on streets–
we could become a very colorful city.
Maybe artistic graffiti as well?

Our street has a roundish intersection –
a T of two streets where one stops.
Great spot for a Milky Way, labyrinth?

For the pre-eclipse festival they will close
the mural street for blocks to celebrate celestial
and earthly delights, encourage biking.

Diabolo for the Solar Eclipse
Diabolo: new poetry form invented by Dennis Turner

Bright diamond ring and Bailey beads
outfit eclipses' daily needs?
Today we'll see.
Like Pac-Man, moon will bite the sun
until the feasting sight is done.
Display beauty?

I sit gob-smacked beneath a tree–
a miracle bequeathed to me?
Solar glasses
'til totality blocks the light.
In our darkness unlocks delight?
More morasses?

After the Solar Eclipse

Is the Fifth Dimension here yet?
Some pundits said after the solar eclipse
we'd witness a transformation, abet
the shift to 5D as our grasp on 3D slips.
        A new reality for us all.
        We'd recreate this 3rd rock ball.

Some pundits said after the solar eclipse
the world would be lighter, more as we dream.
Will we experience much fewer blips?
How different will our lives seem?
        Will our DNA re-arrange, tweak?
        How I'd like to sneak a peek!

We'd witness a transformation, abet
our evolution into a cosmic plan,
move forward without regret,
into an enlightened galactic clan.
        If it happened, I did not feel it.
        Might take awhile for cosmos to reveal it?

The shift to 5D as our grasp on 3D slips,
will demand adjustments, many unaware
how our consciousness flips
to a new world, when old world is not there.
        Are we ready? Of good conscience?
        What are the conditions? Enough resilience?

A new reality for us all
where love, peace and compassion reigns,
living by a new protocol
in totally refurbished domains.
        We've heard of utopias before.
        Is this another illusion more?

We'd recreate this 3rd rock ball
into a sustainable planet, treated with respect--
we're high-minded, downright celestial.
Maybe then we can galactically re-connect,
        become a cosmic citizen,
        a universal 5D denizen?

Synchronicity

Sometimes when something surprising occurs,
you think perhaps there is a multiversal plan.
Actually some energetic force prefers
to see connections link and they can--
       be serendipitous, bring delight?
       Sometimes things go right.

You think perhaps there is a multiversal plan
and each of us is a starseed ort with a contract.
This earthly experiment is part of a cosmic clan
designed to dream and interact
       in ways to bring happiness, love
       co-ordinated from above?

Actually some energetic force prefers
to advance consciousness, provide perks,
to deliver free will with bonus offers?
How frabjous when synchronicity works!
       We find our son at an art show,
       without any of us in the know.

To see connections link and they can
while together we strolled, enjoy the art--
jeweler, wood carver, painter, glass artisan.
Laughing, appreciating, taking part
       in Labor Day sun before the heat.
       Purchases made the event complete.

Be serendipitous, bring delight
to experience texture, color, design!
The timing was perfect. What insight
brought us there so paths align?
       A painting will enrich son's desk.
       My decoupage angel is loftily picturesque.

Sometimes things go right
and happen inevitably?
Sometimes darkness shifts to light?
Uplifting as life is supposed to be?
       Today's unexpected pleasure
       enhanced my mood beyond measure.

Spiral

Everything turns in circles and spirals
with the cosmic heart until infinity.
Everything has a vibration
that spirals inward and outward—
and everything turns together
in the same direction
at the same time.
This vibration keeps going.
It becomes born and expands
or closes and destructs—
only to repeat the cycle again
in the opposite current...
Such is the story of the sun and moon,
of me and you. Nothing truly dies.
All energy simply transforms.

Suzy Kassem

Spirals

Spirals are a world-wide graphic symbol
related to the circle, especially concentric circle systems
but both symbols have different interpretations.

The spiral is a dynamic system with a movement
of rolling up (involution) or unwinding (evolution)
center-outward, outside inward.

Considered macroscopic movement of flowing energy
in the winding fog of the cosmos
invisible to the naked eye.

A schematic image of the evolution of the universe,
symbolizes the orbit of the moon,
rotation of the Earth.

Complex meanings include cyclic development
of moon phases and their influence
on water and fertility, etc.

A dynamic symbol of life force and microcosmic:
galaxies, whirlwinds, whirlpools, coiled serpents,
conical shells and human fingerprints.

Cosmic forms in motion
the relationship between unity
and multiplicity.

Spiral has been associated with sinking
into the "waters of death" used on megalithic graves,
or to movement of the stars through night sky.

Petroglyphs are struck by sun rays through a crack
in the structure on solstices in particular,
related to notions of death and resurrection.

A double spiral indicates the movement
of involution and evolution of the cosmos as a whole,
return and renewal like a labyrinth and DNA in every cell.

A symbol of growth, the snake
as symbol of wisdom and eternity
in Egyptian hieroglyphs and Hebrew *vau*.

Three forms of spiral: expanding like nebula
contracting like a whirlpool
or ossified like a snail's shell.

First form is an active sun symbol
and the second and third cases
a negative moon-symbol.

Most theorists agree the spiral symbolism
is complex and of doubtful origin,
relates to lunar animals and to water.

A creative spiral rises clockwise, Pallas Athene
destructive spiral like a whirlwind
is a Poseidon attribute.

It can be the center of spider's web
represent the Kundalini force
of Tantric doctrine like a snake.

Spiral symbolism motifs in ornamental art
all around the world: curve curling up from given point,
scrolls, or sigmas, back to prehistoric art.

Celtic double spirals, volutes on Roman columns,
whorls in Maori carving, tattooing in South Pacific.
Spiral motifs are more often unconscious than conscious.

Potter's wheel spirals are produced by an object
spinning through damp clay. Mere doodling.
Not sure of any significance.

A double spiral could be in pubic area triangle
of Neolithic "mother goddess" statuette.
Romanesque sculpture–double spiral in Christ's garment folds.

Prehistoric burial structures have triple spirals
whose significance we do not know.   A difficult path
in and out again in tradition of death and rebirth?

Megalithic spirals suggest a journey to the afterlife
and perhaps a return. Snakes on caduceus
suggest a balance of opposing principles.

The yin-yang symbol, vortex forces in wind,
water and fires suggest ascent, descent
of rotating energy that drives the cosmos.

Symbol of a hurricane- creative and destructive
like functions in the universe, suspension
of provisional, but pacific order of the universe.

Spiral can symbolize time, cyclic rhythms
of seasons, birth and death, waning and waxing moon,
and the sun also symbolized by a spiral.

There is a connection to breathing
and the creative breath of life symbolizing
breath and spirit. Rhythm of life itself.

Egyptian god Thoth wears spiral on his head.
Significance is connection with creation, movement
and progressive development, also power of Pharaoh.

Found in *lituus* of Roman augurs
and walking sticks today. Relationship
of circle and the center.

Like yogic "serpent" at the base of the spine,
spring-like-coil suggests latent power.
Uncoiling spiral is male, involuted is female.

Spiral is associated with dance-- primitive dances
of healing and incantation. Movement develops
a spiral curve, circle to center and out.

The spiral is open and flowing line,
suggests extension, evolution, continuity
and centripetal movement.

Spiral patterns in mandalas and European figures
intended to induce a state of ecstasy to escape the material world
to beyond through "hole" symbolized by mystic center.

Striking spirals found at Gravinas (Moribihan)
New Grange (Leinster), Carnwath (Scotland)
Castle Archdall (Ulster).

Single and double spirals were most sacred signs
of Neolithic Europe, on megalithic monuments and temples,
Spiral *oculi* double twist resemble eyes, on ionic columns.

A spiral labyrinth common from Finland to Cornwall
Crete to Chartres, in the Americas, and as serpent
guardians of Sumerian temples.

Labyrinth designs decorate cathedrals,
magic staff *lituus* used by diviners
marked out sacred areas in temple sites.

Spirals are connected to idea of death and rebirth,
entering mysterious earth womb, penetrating to the core
and passing out again the same route.

Myths say the universe begins with roundness,
the spiral is one of the symbols to express a human
sense of the wholeness of things, circular nature of things

Definitions of spiral from
Dictionary of Symbolism, Hans Biedermann
a dictionary of symbols, j.e. cirlot
The Herder Symbol Dictionary, Boris Matthews
Dictionary of Symbols, Jack Tresidder
Woman's Symbols and Sacred Objects, Barbara G. Walker

Portals

Spirals twisting in our DNA
      wiggle-worming through worm holes,
            hurricanes, those enormous spinning tops
that topple, gobble all in its path.

Twirling on weather's merry-go-round
      like a planetary orbit following patterns
           punctured by glistening satellites
              probed by space craft
and peeked upon by space telescopes.

All destined for the big gulp of a black hole?
      Or perhaps winding into the black maw
           to be spit out anew in new configurations
           or from a singularity
              as omniversal orts
      in multiversal galaxies
spiraling new genesis.

A Hard Time

It's a hard time to be human. We know too much and too little. Ellen Bass

We know too much to know better.
We know too little to do better.

Technology changes the way we communicate,
build, create and devastate.

Old beliefs don't keep up with advances.
New ideas bring hopeful chances.

Mired in waste and pollution,
we are too slow with a solution.

We destroy Earth while searching the sky.
People suffering, need more help, more to try.

Art, science, philosophy, spirituality
present different views on reality.

What are we to do with Gaia's stardust stuff?
Whatever we learn it is not enough.

Hands

Sometimes, reaching out
and taking someone's hand
is the beginning of a journey.

Vera Nazarian

Getting to the Root of Things

My new massage therapist
is a wonder with hands and stones,
energizing chakras, keeping
my body toasty and moist.

She suggested an energetic
spring cleaning of my chakras.
I was smooth sailing from head (crown)
(white) to middling by orange (sacral)
and muddy by the red root chakra.

Apparently amid the pink ball
in the root chakra, I had some black
threads or root-lets that needed
be pulled, dug out. I was not
attaching fully with the Earth
and I needed some negativity
rooted out to plant more fully.

I am an avid advocate for Gaia,
all her creatures, all her attributes,
but I am not actively tree-hugging,
hiking, gardening, sun-bathing.
I am a pale, blue-eyed, arthritic
crone who gets skin cancer
if exposed to too much sun.

But I joined in trying to release
energy through my feet and cleanse
my root chakra with visualizing
pink strands and yanking out
the black ones. Reminded me
of the Violet Flame technique
when the shaman netted
all my gunk and plunked it into
the ground.

I have always believed I was
loosely attached to the Earth,
floating like a balloon, tethered
by my grounding husband.
I like being a lighter being,
for my heavy physical body
often causes me pain.

Perhaps getting to the root
of my malaise by clearing
my energetic spinning chakras
will rev up healing energy.
I might connect more easily
to the earth and my body
when it is not so painful.

I listen to a CD before
sleeping which with exotic music
and a droning guru induces
sleep while stirring my chakras.
Often I am asleep by blue.
We start with red, the root chakra
so it gets the first most alert attention,
yet blue (throat) through white (top of head)
is my clearest channel?

At my next massage we need to do
another root chakra session.
How long will I be in remedial
treatment? When will I accept
the Earth's conditions and connect
more closely or will I continue
to dwell in my mind in the cosmos?

Honey's Hands

Everyone called my mother Honey,
even her children and grandchildren.
The name fit her in every way
but one–her hands.

Her handiwork in crafts, needlework,
interior design, writing, cooking–
anything she did with her hands
was excellent–had the Honey touch.

But as she aged, her hands
had deep wrinkles, brown age spots,
fingers curled with arthritis, her crooked hands,
she called witch's hands.

Our young son stroked her hands
and said "So sad, do they hurt?"
She appreciated his kindness–
but not the condition of her hands.

After her death in a dream
we were together in her living room.
She showed me her smooth, unblemished hands–
she said, "Look, they are so beautiful."

Hand Designs

A glistening bubble on my right pinky,
looks gelatinous, solid,--
seems to have a black dot.
Everyone suggested it's a wart.

Fearing more skin cancer--
cancery like my nose was,
I finally consulted a dermatologist.
It's a digital mucous cyst.

No idea why we get them.
Few ideas how to cure them.
Could use electricity zap, but
they return. Just bad luck.

But they are benign and painless,
a nubby nuisance, unpleasant protrusion.
On my right thumb a companion,
at this point a pimple, emerges.

My pinky cyst is near a joint
and would need surgery
for careful removal–but ganglions
could still return the bubble.

I am not to burst the bubble
as it could get infected. Just learn
to live with it, avoid disturbing
the tadpole-like embryo with black eye.

The doctor said it was about as big
as the pinky pop-up will go.
The thumb bump will grow
and I can just watch cyst rising.

My hands have wrinkle patterns,
age spots, why not cysts?
So far no arthritis and loss of function.
So why not some texture, shiny lumps?

Playing Scrabble with English Teachers

Today we had a full contingent of six.
We have played together for years.
We have many lives to probe and fix.
Times for joy, laughter and tears.
       These gals play by the rules.
       They come equipped with tools.

We have played together for years
before and after most have retired.
They play boldly, overcome fears
for winning is what most have desired.
       But I do not care about the score.
       With me, a great word counts more.

We have many lives to probe and fix
not just ours, but for generations.
Oh! the relationships we would nix!
Ah! the sensational revelations!
       We know each other very well,
       what we think and how we spell.

Times for joy, laughter and tears.
Today one recovering from foot surgery.
Other problems still in arrears.
All oppose the Trump insurgency.
       We are liberal feminists–without doubt,
       discussing issues inside and out.

These gals play by the rules
unlike my cooperative poet Scrabble pals.
These players obey when Scrabble book overrules.
Keep things on board and remain rational
       I like free-wheeling Scrabble better,
       when we can innovate, unfetter.

They come equipped with tools
and knowledge gleaned over years of play.
They even play on-line in high-skill pools.
It's still fun to wile stimulating hours away.
       We learn so much when English teachers dabble
       in a competitive, pensive game of Scrabble.

Venting Scrabble

After another Trump disaster for global environment--
just after "covfefe" and this day's destruction of progress,
our cooperative Scrabble group, feeling depressed
by the daily deluge of bad and fake news,
decided to vent by finding anti-Trump words.

We play nine-tile, non-scoring games,
cooperatively and move from board
to the table cloth after the first round.
We make patterns, use dictionaries, assist,
and found many persist and resist protest words.

After four games we had compiled a long list--
many impolite, slightly scandalous, very appropriate
to us, but maybe not to all factions of the nation.
We could laugh at his gaffs, but our hearts were heavy.
We tried to uplift our dispirited Huddle souls.

Scrabble in times of Trump words were: depose, bozo,
zero, blab, idiot, cowardly, motives, money, price, counter,
guilt, toasted, stroke, touch, voted, caution, afraid,
toxin, tomb, coffer, bragged, lagged, unduly, blown,
punned, bouncer, penalty, bitterly, wrack, foxfire.

Looking at the chaos of letters and ordering them,
tile by tile, word by word– seeking words for the theme
added to the challenge and helped release our anger.
Lining up our words opposing his, empowers us
to keep up the resistance and work for justice.

Balloons

Balloons don't only burst at pop concerts,
they billow and blow skyward after birthdays
and graduations. Balloons celebrate.

Balloons shape into glistening words,
or become confetti-filled like a pinata,
Mother's Day and Valentine's balloons deflate.

Balloons to sky-ride, to inflate in space,
to cuddle-comfort a crying child,
to propose or to toss and play with.

Balloons released take flight out of sight--
a happy, hope symbol, like a crystal ball
to bring clarity to those holding the strings.

Rock Creations

My grandmother lined her garden paths with rocks.
My husband built yard walls with sidewalk chunks.
These were not painted, but natural stone boundaries.

The Kindness Rock Project paints inspirational
messages on rocks, left for individuals to find
in parks, parking lots, paths or install as rock gardens.

In rock gardens people can pick the message
that resonates, but the random rocks of kindness
perk up spirits when found along their way.

We had pet rocks as a fad once. Rock throwing,
stoning women or skimming water was mostly
a guy thing. Now we have rocks of kindness.

Perhaps we need boulders, positive graffiti
to display messages of love and kindness
to connect to forces of support and empowerment.

Public stone sculptures, architectural marvels,
embellished or not, rocks rock our world,--
even rock and roll. Rocka my soul.

Monolithic messages from ancient cultures need translation.
Petroglyphs–images of hands and spirit beings intrigue.
Mountains and canyons drop-jaw awe.

Kindness rocks are hold-able, manageable,
uplifting creations. Maybe I'll imprint poetry rocks,
line the front wall with rock poems.

You could pick from my poetry rock garden. Probably
a lot of haiku, unless a slab–leftover counter-top granite?
A rock scroll could invite inscriptions with permanent markers.

Rock painting parties, rock readings, rock testimonials,
steles of inspiration, chalk on sidewalks and playgrounds...
Let's not get carried away and 3D print plastic rocks.

Gum Walls

In Portland at the base of a vacant building,
a historic landmark on Couch Street
a gum mural will replace a favorite
urinating spot for a tourist attraction.
The foot traffic good to boost business
for a tattoo parlor near Old Town Chinatown.

For $20 worth of gum, customers
received a $150 voucher toward tattoo work.
The owner collects the gum and gives it away
to chewers to create an urban art gum wall,
part of "Keep Portland Weird". Perhaps
gummers can clean up the neighborhood.

Bubblegum Alley in San Luis Obispo
inspired Seattle in 1993 to create
Market Theater Post Alley gum wall
under the Pike Street Market,
power-washed after 20 years.
In November 2015.

Post Alley was the second germiest
tourist attraction after the Blarney Stone.
To cease erosion of bricks from sugar,
the tourist spot was steamed clean
in fruity, minty wafting air,
so re-gumming could start anew.

2350 pounds of gum globs
in 94 gallon buckets,
from a 50 foot long, 15 foot high wall--
de-gummed. Some gum had coins
plunked in the gum globs.
How did they recycle the gum gobs this time?

In Portland public gum-art participation
is better than public urination, creating
a colorful mosaic, textured brick wall.
I'll pass on chewing for gum graffiti,
risk of pulling ancient fillings from their spots,
for blobbing wads gumming up walls.

Chalk on the Sidewalk
> *Life with love is better.* Sidewalk chalk message written in Arabic in
> Corvallis by Shurooq Alblushi visiting from Oman.

In our town we have hopscotch
and chalk art contests–light-expressions
on the sidewalks, mostly erased by rain.

In our town some anonymous messages
appeared–ugly, racist rhetoric, words
quickly removed by Public Works.

In our town several progressive groups,
CARE (Community Action for Racial Equality)
SUR (Showing Up for Racial Justice) responded

to the hate chalk talk with colorful art and positive
affirmations. All ages crouched and crawled
to scrawl language of inclusion and love.

Strength in diversity. Teach tolerance.
Open minds. Open hearts. Hate-free Zone.
Tell everyone on the train I love them

last repeating what Taliesin Myrddin Namkai-Meche
said before stabbed to death on Max train
defending two teen girls against racist remarks.

In the neighboring town when the city
government did not include "equity"
and "diversity" in city code– they marched.

Over 550 joined the town's first Pride March,
in support and unity for the message
"We are all equal."

Amid the flags, costumes, chants-
on the sidewalk in colorful chalk
among the messages--

> *You are loved,*
> *you are welcome*
> *you are supported.*

Chalk is not a permanent marker.

The Pendant

The final forming of a person's character lies in their own hands. Anne Frank

Anne's forming was taken out of her hands
by the Nazis, but her diaries,
written in her own hand remain
to reveal her shining character.

Born in the same year 1929 in Frankfort
a German Jewish girl Karoline Cohn
suffered the same fate at Sobibor
along with 250,000 others.

Anne and Karoline wore the same pendant.
No other pendant like these have been found.
Researchers are trying to discover
if Anne and Karoline were related.

The pendant is a triangle saying
Mazal Tov, Heh the Jewish letter
for God's name, three stars of David
and Karoline's birth date.

Cattle cars filled with people
were gassed on arrival, now
they are trying to unearth what happened
at Sorbibor–piece by piece.

The Nazis stole teeth fillings, jewelry,
hair, clothes– anything from their victims
that could aid their twisted cause.
The pendant remains–a reminder.

The final forming of Nazis' character
was in their hands...for them to live with
while the Allies took things into their hands
to expose evil's handiwork.

Re-Wiring the World

Still I mourn...the era when one's voice was an isolated incident, as it were, an
isolated instrument for sure. When the phone call was a tunnel to hearts,
minds, souls even. When it was just us with our voices, and a ringing.
Strawberry Saroyan

I don't mourn it—I still live it.
No cell phone–just land line.
No Facebook, Twitter, Snapchat.
No face to face imaging.
I can have a bad hair day or rash
and nobody would see...or care.

Telephone poles and cell towers
stake the landscape–quantum waves
waft through us. Wired and wireless
communication- smart and dumb phones.
I have the plugged land line, sightless variety.
Re-purpose the telephone equipment?
Maybe decorate poles and towers?

My computer can use Skype, if I want.
e-mail, Internet, all kinds of connections
not on my phone are accessible.
No apps, but plenty of ways to connect
and communicate, explore with wonder.

My resistance is my lack of nerdiness
to figure out how to handle and use
a more advanced phone. They fascinate me,
but when I touch them, try to type, try
to learn how to actually operate them—nada.
I am technologically inept, phone-tically Luddite.

I have to explore other media, other screens.
I carry a mobile phone around the house
and keep it near me to reduce rushing to rings.
When I venture into outside, I am phone-less,
computer-less, un-wired. Many types of operators
with various equipment do not have to feel alone.
A fingertip away the wired and un-wired world
can enhance and create your personal reality.

My hand-held device pushes buttons.
Touch and stick poking phones–bamboozle.
Guess I need a voice-command device,
then I'm in command until a solar flare.

Acts of Kindness

It's a simple way to put good out there. It builds community. People feel good when they're doing it. It's just this magical thing.
Megan Murphy on The Kindness Rock Project

When situations look dire and people desire
to make the world a kinder place,
movements for kindness provoke action, inspire
the best instincts of the human race.
    Acts of kindness can be direct--
    second-hand, with no suspect.

To make the world a kinder place
people build boxes for free books or food.
Sometimes its encouragement face to face
to provide a healthy, safe space,
    building community and connection
    by a compassionate selection.

Movements for kindness provoke action, inspire
all ages to collect Fund Me sites for self or others.
Tragedies lead victors and victims to aspire
to a better way for all sisters and brothers.
    Charities, foundations gather resources
    but individuals also re-steer their courses.

The best instincts of the human race
expressed in art and tender word,
try to reach out, hope commonplace,
as they desperately want to be heard.
    Those whose hearts and mind respond
    seize the present and look beyond.

Acts of kindness can be direct
taking someone's hand, touching a heart.
Providing care, thoughtful gestures, inject
a dose of laughter, support, become a part
    of someone's life, make things better:
    a visit, a meal, a call, a letter.

Second-hand, with no suspect
money appears in products, rock
paintings with upbeat messages effect
darkness with starlight to unlock
    love and caring so we can hope.
    Acts of kindness help us cope.

Healing

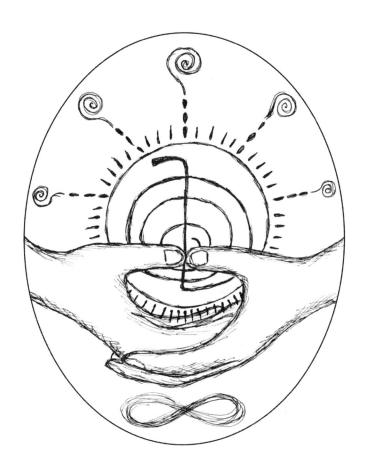

The wound is the place
where the Light enters you...

If you desire healing,
let yourself fall ill.
Let yourself fall ill.

Jalaluddin Rumi

Ancient Healing

We're guided. We listen to our heart. We're just given knowledge from word of mouth. We listen. We know what it means when our body gives us discomfort. We know what to do to take care of it. We seem to be connected to the earth. We used to remember how to heal the earth. Dolores Cannon

Past life regressions give insights into ancient healing.
Natural healing is making a comeback.
What can we learn from ancestral healers?

By meditation, ancestors created harmony
for people, realized they were all connected.
They used herbs and shared knowledge communally.

If anything we ever learned is never lost,
but stored in the subconscious mind, it could
be brought forth if appropriate for our time?

What techniques, rituals, ingredients, mindsets
can we glean from the past and from the universe
to prevent suffering and damage to us and Gaia?

Current healing traditions can learn from each other.
Some ancient practices have survived until today.
Some methods can avoid pain and surgery.

Ancient healers used earth materials
sought guidance from the cosmos,
listened to balance and harmonize their lives.

Healing Energy

My new masseuse has magic hands.
Sometimes she glides my skin with stones.
Somehow her being understands
what is rattling around my bones.
        My chakras need brightening.
        My energy needs lightening.

Sometimes she glides my skin with stones,
so warm and slithery and healing.
Somehow my body aligns, atones
and stops the chaotic reeling.
        She adds heated pads to places
        where increasing energy races.

Somehow her being understands
how energy flows and is out of whack.
She senses vibrations with her hands
and moves light to where I lack
        the frequency to make it move,
        restores some joy and love.

What is rattling around my bones
is arthritis, toxins, crumbling parts.
I'm indebted to the gifted ones
who practice the healing arts.
        My body relaxes, but not total leisure
        the kneading, pushing-- I feel pressure.

My chakras need brightening
since a foggy funk clouds my soul.
Clearing dark spots is enlightening.
She plays a detective role.
        Chakras spin. We persist,
        finally call angels to assist.

My energy needs lightening
from the heaviness of this 3D world.
Perhaps it's grip is tightening
before the 5D reality is unfurled.
        Until then I'll try to stay in shape
        and resist the urgency to escape.

Health is Your Wealth

Even when you're frustrated, or confused, or simply can't get where you're being lead...just relax, trust, and all things will happen as they are destined for your Highest Possibility. Sara Wiseman

Another frustrating, disappointing doctor visit
where he just did not listen to my concerns--
(I had read about curing my health symptoms)
not the response this patient yearns.

The internet is full of gurus'--cures for a price.
Jean Houston unlocks your Quantum Powers.
Shimoff and Poneman offer a Miraculous Life.
Bob Doyle bridges Abundance Gap, empowers.

All the miraculous solutions to heal mind, body, soul.
Can't afford to try them all. Lucky some videos free.
But I'm just reading about so many possibilities--
while still feeling poorly as healing escapes me.

Dr. Izabella Wentz promotes the Thyroid Secret.
All kinds of tests and lists of symptoms.
T4 and T3, dietary changes, stem cell, laser therapy.
Look for a Functional Doctor for better outcomes.

Neale Donald Walsh in conversing with God
suggests self-realization and self-confidence connect.
Expand understanding why we're here and for what.
True self is individualized divinity. We've miracles to perfect.

Dr. Bruce Lipton advocates epigenetics.
Your beliefs not genes cause disease progression.
Your mind, consciousness, how you see world,
environmental signals change gene expression.

Brad Lemley promotes wild-caught, oily fish
for best Omega 3 with wondrous claims.
(In earlier times and Last Supper they ate less polluted fish).
His Ultra Omega expensive pills fulfill aims.

The trick seems to take control of your health,
change diet, life style, beliefs, find updated doctor.
I've spent more time on brain and soul, not body.
I wonder who will be the next miraculous concoctor?

Not Simpatico With Sciatica

My first trip to a chiropractor–
prompted by sharp sciatica pain--
like left leg and hip clasped by a raptor.
I needed to walk and sleep again.
       I had no idea what to expect.
       My acupuncturist suggested who to select.

Prompted by sharp sciatica pain,
irritated, I filled out several pages.
Visions of my credit card drain.
I wait while my considerable pain rages.
       All of a sudden he was there.
       I rolled toward him in my wheel chair.

Like left leg and hip clasped by a raptor,
he pulled muscles with a push and a pop.
I was his agonized victim, he my captor.
I wished the increased torture would stop.
       He said my legs were the same length now.
       My crooked pelvis re-aligned somehow.

I needed to walk and sleep again
so I winced with hope at each pull and prod.
For teeth they give you novocain,
this was an unmedicated path to trod.
       He lifted each leg up to his shoulder,
       then swung them outward. I'm stunned beholder.

I had no idea what to expect.
I was stretching like an athlete.
Was this helping? I was suspect.
But I was accomplishing this feat.
       Then relaxed on rolling "happy" bed,
       I'm pummeled gently from lower back to head.

My acupuncturist suggested who to select
and as a result I became better each day.
He un-pinched my nerve, so I could correct
alignments and move in less painful way.
       I'll return twice more for reassurance,
       visits mostly paid for by insurance.

Mobility

I used to meditate in my backyard–
an inquisitive cancered-nosy bard,
who finds this rocky planet hard.

I sat facing dawn in a lawn chair
with a notebook, alert and aware
sneaker-ed feet should not be bare.

A fair-weather mediator
I moved inside by window, radiator--
soft chair, dark chocolate conciliator.

Indoors, my cosmically curious mind
seeks any comfort it can find
and hopes the multiverse is kind.

I am having trouble getting around.
Aging body tends to confound.
Flighty ideas need to ground.

In motorized cart, grocery shoppers beware!
I attend some events in a wheelchair,
grateful I can get around out there.

I dwell far from the state of beatitude,
looking with upwardly mobile attitude
trying to obtain cosmic gratitude.

Aging Imposes Changes

People can relate to the human reality of letting go and losing something, and then re-establishing a part of yourself.
Wendy Wheland, former ballerina finding new home in dance at 50.

As we age, bodily and situational changes--
they urge us to let go of the past, invent a new future.
As a relationship or a body part re-arranges,
we're to re-establish, slice or suture.
>Things don't work the way they did before.
>Is phoenix an appropriate metaphor?

They urge us to let go of the past, invent a new future
re-envision our capabilities and our destiny.
Re-assess the demands of commitments and culture,
all the while your body is in mutiny.
>Will our minds stay clear to do the task?
>For direction, who do we ask?

As a relationship or a body part re-arranges,
our efforts to sustain and nourish can strain
resources and contacts, our attempt estranges,
causes you and others considerable pain or gain.
>What once held true might not work
>in a reconsidered framework or network.

We're to re-establish, slice or suture
choose to re-create, sever, or repair.
What is worth the energy expenditure
or expenses of what you share?
>As we form a new directive,
>we must be more selective.

Things don't work the way they did before.
New ailments, new connections' expectations.
Working with less, you want to do more.
What will happen after your reflections?
>Age can bring wisdom...or not.
>Retain what you haven't forgot?

Is phoenix an appropriate metaphor-
rising from ashes, renewed for new try?
Will you strengthen a vital core?
Will you rise to challenges and begin to fly?
>I am a light-chasing, word-playing work in progress,
>wondering if my transformation will be a success.

Modifying My Mobile Work Station

My gray walker with a tray
is a multi-purpose work station.
My four-legged pet walks with me
all around the house—two paws
are yellow tennis balls.

I should name this constant companion,
who eats, walks and sits with me.
The tray and legs hold water, food,
writing supplies, and other convenient items.
I add decorations and enhancements.

The front has a smile of Tibetan prayer flags
looped above a fabric, black, brief case
which contains paper, books, notes, napkins.
One side holds red and yellow exercise bands
and a hand towel. Both sides have bike streamers.

Stuck in the other side is a two-toned pinwheel
which whirs if parallel and is out of the way when
when watching TV. My newest modification
is an old, brown belly pack with three zippers, one holds
pens, another unworn glasses, third-dark chocolate.

My next addition might be rainbow tape
to cover the gray and make a calico cat type pet.
During exercise class a tray-less, fold-able,
unadorned walker with a hanging bag for weights,
band, and red membership card waits at my side.

This walker rides in the car and is not really
my work station-- more a support contrivance
to keep me vertical, balanced and knees
from yowling. Maybe this walker should
be colorfully taped, to match the draped bag?
But like the wheelchair, not used very much.

My main work station away from the computer
waits patiently as I pluck at the computer keys.
Adorned in colorful garb she is a topic of conversation
during a meeting here as she holds my gear.
I think I'll call her Patience—which I need much more of.
Next modification should be me.

Gussied Up Walker

To balance and prevent possible falls
I have a gussied up, four- legged walker--
two legs have wheels, two--tennis balls.
I'm a slow-gaited, assisted stalker,
     carrying prey upon its tray,
     room to room in a convenient way.

I have a gussied, four-legged walker--
and plain one with seat for outside as well.
I can sit and listen to any talker
and my knees don't ache or yell.
     In the drooping pouch beneath the seat
     I carry purse, needed things or a treat.

Two legs have wheels, two–tennis balls,
on my other inside smooth gliding device.
Light aluminum frame prevents pratfalls.
My movements become more precise.
     I like to decorate supports for each season,
     to brighten up gray for a joyous reason.

I am a slow-gaited, assisted stalker
pushing my garnished walker to a destination.
When it comes to color I'm no balk-er
and fussy up metal skeleton with flaring imagination.
     A fabric brief case, lobs over front bar,
     toting books, paper, pens–spectacular.

Carrying prey upon its tray
I transport drinks, food, pills on cleared surface.
Two exercise stretch bands dangle and sway,
row of Tibetan prayer flags, towel for hands and face.
     Bike streamers button to flow from both sides--
     hearts, pinks, blues with black polka dots with my strides.

Room to room in a convenient way,
I ferry add-ons and drop offs to right spot.
I am puppeteer of props as I work and play.
I am charioteer of my overloaded, garish chariot.
     I swish place to place well-stocked and aware.
     My colorful fanfare parades with me everywhere.

Not Brought to My Knees Yet

My
knee-jerk
reaction
does tend to be
fear.

Both
knees ache
lack balance
when plan to stand
up.

Not
on my
knees, must sit,
use walker to
stalk.

I
march in
wheelchair to
persist, resist
Trump.

No
matter
condition
of my knees, I
move.

Move
for change!
If can't walk–
roll on forward–
Now!

Until the Last Hurrah

To write something you have to risk making a fool of yourself. Anne Rice

I once was a lean, limber lass.
I scored at the top of my class,
shaped like thin hour-glass.
　　　'Twas then, alas. 'Twas then, alas.

My mobility is less now.
But manage to word-play somehow.
This arthritic, lumbering cow—
　　　shouts "ow" and "wow". Shouts "ow" and "wow"!

Creativity

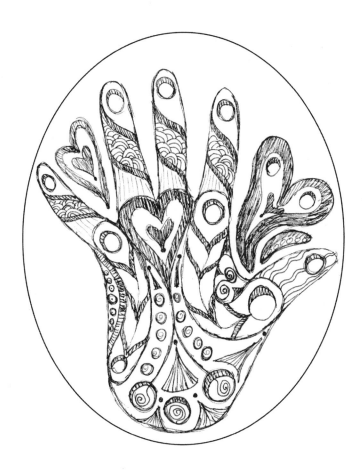

*Rational thoughts never
drive people's creativity
the way emotions do.*

Neil deGrasse Tyson

Imagination

Imagination is what makes each of us uniquely human but also what allows us to live cooperatively with others in a wider natural world that is relentlessly coming at you in high speed. We neglect imagination at our own peril.
Stephen T. Asma

Since childhood my source of fascination
is the power of imagination
to empower knowledge and innovation.

Imagination is the source of invention,
putting old beliefs into detention,
discover new thoughts for attention.

Imagination can build civilizations,
help us explore imponderable realizations,
take us to surreal destinations.

Imagination is the creative spark
bringing light into the dark,
finding different ways to embark.

Imagination is multidimensional,
our access can be intentional
a given gift, result exponential.

Imagination helps me find meaning
from all the data I'm gleaning,
sweeps my mind for shining cleaning.

Imagination is a prime priority
even in my increasing seniority.
I appreciate its cosmic enormity.

Granny Smith: Not Just Apples

Passion is one great force that unleashes creativity, because when you're passionate about something then you're more willing to take risks. Yo-Yo Ma

This Granny Smith is not an apple, but
a passionate, curiosity seeker,
word-player who can't keep eyes and mouth shut.
I'm an often risky peeker.
      I want people to expand and question.
      People don't need to accept my suggestion.

A passionate, curiosity seeker
I want to push boundaries, climb outside the box.
Probably considered a real geek-her.
I like to find what I can out-fox.
      I want to be free of fear,
      to let light appear.

Word-player who can't keep eyes and mouth shut--
eyes tear, mouthing what is a guess,
eagerly search out another's input.
Wonderful when you can high-five and yowl yes!
      We want to connect, discover love,
      but passions get dampened and get a shove.

I'm often a risky peeker
into the cosmos and fantastical realms,
try to talk with an understanding speaker,
not greasing palms or pressuring alms.
      Magical creatures are everywhere.
      I want to meet them, become aware.

I want people to expand and question,
commit to an idea that resonates,
be open, hold thoughts in suspension.
Who is in charge? Who regulates?
      Create new projects, keep informed.
      Discard your rejects, if ill - informed.

People don't need to accept my suggestion.
Everyone scripts their own story.
I just hope we pay attention,
perhaps lead us to a higher dimensional glory?
      Passion is broader than lust--
      inflame us toward trust and what's just.

Poetic Urges

We all need poetry. The moments in our lives that characterized by language that has to do with necessity or the market or just, you know things that take us away from the big questions that we have, those are the things that I think urge us to think about what a poem can offer. Tracy K. Smith

Poetic urges take me beyond boundaries,
to question earthly and cosmic quests.
I seek no limits to my curiosity
and follow what my intuition requests.

Issues of the heart and mind
can exist from above or below.
If reality is a holographic illusion,
I persist in wanting to know.

Poetry serves necessity and fantasy
finds surprises, new ways to confide,
new possibilities to explore,
reveals what people tend to hide.

Poetry urges images and sounds to manifest
powerfully as the poet's language is expressed.

Letting Go of Poems

A poem asks you to let go many of your assumptions, move away from your own certainties and to listen. Tracy K. Smith

Whether reading or writing a poem,
you wonder how words will create a line,
what ideas will find a home,
hope it will all come out fine.
      Will the ideas conform
      to any semblance of form?

You wonder how words will create a line
and then how they will glob into stanzas.
At any stage does the poem outline
intentions to build into a bonanza?
      Some lines limp along,
      never becoming sharp and strong.

What ideas will find a home
from inside your buzzy head?
Will they continue to roam
or settle into place instead?
      Does the poem grab you, lasso
      your attention and puzzle you?

Hope it will all come out fine
and if it doesn't try again, then abandon.
Not all poems and audiences align.
Move on to a craftier phenomenon.
      Assume you might learn something new
      though perhaps it doesn't agree with you.

Will the ideas conform
to your expectations or challenge your assumptions?
Poems do not always perform
to readers or poets preferred presumptions.
      Poets deal with a free-spirited muse,
      who brings considerations hard to refuse.

To any semblance of form
do these whisks of words line up?
Let go and let poems inform?
Sip and drink in like from a coffee cup?
      I let poems have their way with me,
      allow me to be delightfully free.

Rap

Is rap a backronym of rhythm and poetry?
The word has a certain snap,
an energy I'd like to tap?

I'd like to give rap music a try--
to speak bluntly, boldly free--,
chatting, chanting, rhythmically.

Do I have enough creativity
to spout rhymed couplets, strike with force
to make conversation change its discourse?

Performing rap, a possibility more
if I could knock out lyrics to rock a dance floor,
then I'd rap revelations for a reviving encore.

Poets in Society

It is the responsibility of society to let the poet be a poet. Grace Paley

Many societies allow one-gender poets' voice.
Some societies rely on the ancient golden-oldies.
Many societies offer a wide-range of choice.
Some societies suggest some poets-- moldy.
　　Short as haiku, long as an epic--
　　poetry can cover any topic.

Some societies rely on the ancient golden-oldies
recording their cultures' myths and history,
how they met their challenges with courage, boldly.
Sappho and so many others remain a mystery.
　　Civilizations come and go,
　　poets go with the flow.

Many societies offer a wide-range of choice,
invent new forms, freed verse, unlock
occasions of sorrow or times to rejoice.
Poets can take own path, don't follow the flock.
　　Poets reflect the societies they live in
　　and artfully share what they're given.

Some societies suggest some poets moldy,
create triple-rhyme rap, all types of lyrics.
Some elements of society review them coldly,
some poets send teens into hysterics.
　　Slam poetry, Nobel poet Bob Dylan,
　　styles come and go with the artisan.

Short as haiku, long as an epic
societies choose poetic expressions.
Poets can keep us from being ethnocentric,
leaving audiences with varied impressions.
　　Poets read from Smart Phones, have web site,
　　keep their listeners' concerns in what they write.

Poetry can cover any topic,
in a free society and attuned audience.
Places that are chaotic, catastrophic--
are less likely have a poetic experience,
　　but poets find a way in some mode.
　　Which societies today deserve an ode?

The Only Rule is No Rules

Go against the rules or ignore the rules, that is what invention is about.
Helen Frankenthaler

After researching over 1000 forms,
writing examples for each of them,
putting them on-line free for others
to word-play and create with,
inventing my own form's rules,
using rules in my own poems...
I discover there are no rules.

Frankenthaler is an artist
who is excited by the unexpected
and by new discoveries as she
used multiple proofs in her printmaking
to explore possibilities. Maybe
I should explore another form of art
as there are no rules to break.

Luckily I never memorized poetry forms,
have references and I practiced enough,
to select a form that might work best
for each poem. Even free verse
was an innovation, which is now
a category of form. I freed myself
from confines of meter, but enjoy
playing with syllabics and rhyme.

Capturing poems into many media,
drawing from nature, human-built
and cosmic environments–even new words
keeps poetry dynamic, unruly, adventurous,
ever-changing–dispensing, upgrading,
re-cogitating rules to toss when they
no longer serve creation.

My First Play

Student teaching in a sixth grade class,
I decided to write a play incorporating
songs and dances. For scene changes,
students would recite a poem.
I remember one memorized "Jabberwocky."

Undaunted, with 20 year old energy
and optimism–I just did it.
I had never written a play,
let alone a musical with dance,
I wrote "Jenny in Storybookland"
where a young girl visited several
classical story settings, sang and danced
with them –everyone had a part.

Many of the children were orphans
whose parents only had to send them
a postcard a year to keep them
from being adopted. They lived
in an orphanage, near the public school.

My mother did not drive and my father
had to drive her to a doctor's appointment.
My parents would not see my debut
as a playwright. One of the few times
my mother let me down. For years
she wondered why she had not changed
her appointment date and come.

To my delight my grandmother
who everyone called "Mom" strolled
down the aisle in a fox stole, its mouth
clenching its tail, as she strutted with a cane.
She had taken the taxi, for she thought
some family should be there for me.
I still see her with that now un-politically
correct fox, almost 60 years later.

My first play had only the one showing
in the auditorium for the whole school.
I wrote a few short plays inside my fantasy
novels, written for little older children.
Now at 77 I am taking an on-line class
through the University of Iowa: Power of the Pen:
Identities and Social Issues in Poetry and Plays.

I have written thousands of poems over the years,
now in these turbulent times, will the turmoil burble
into a longer, non-musical play? My first play
was full of joy, delight, hope–potential happiness.
It was a fantasy world, more believable than now.

Before I attempt a second play, I should dig out
the browning pages of my first play, to recall
a time when my grandmother traipsed with a fox,
though disappointed in my mother- I recovered,
and saw happy children acting, singing and dancing
with promises of clear sky and rainbows.

Despite Vigils and Vows
It is with poetry as with Chess and Billiards–There is a certain degree of attainment,
which practice will reach, and beyond which no vigils and vows will go.
John Quincy Adams

JQA punished himself for being a mediocre poet.
His Puritan heritage made him scold himself
for the poor quality of his verse.

I do not write poetry for fame or greed.
I word-play to explore the cosmos.
I don't judge my word-smithery.

In critique groups I do not rank a poem,
but work with others to create a better poem.
The result is up to anyone's opinion.

For over 30 years, I read thousands of poems,
yearly to select and discuss with other editors
which poems most effectively shared Calyx's mission.

It was a chance to read women's poetry
after years of force-read mostly men's poetry
which I was to critique for class credit.

I never read JQA's poems, so I do not know
if I would agree with his self-assessment.
I did not resonate with a lot of male canon.

When *No More Masks* and the Women's movement
published more women's poetry, women won prizes,
shed male pen names, could be judged by own rules.

My favorite poet is May Swenson. She just happens
to be well-respected, but I like her for her imaginative
word-experiments and delightful sense of humor.

When I teach poetry I present prompts and possible forms
students can plunk their poems into. I encourage the process
attempts, not the quality of product-- when I had to grade.

When I attend poetry classes and workshops, I come
to learn new approaches, what poets are concerned about,
how they deal with today's turbulence, discover new poets.

Free to read any poet I want to read, I don't select by
book blurbs, go by book critics-- I pick them off bookshelves,
gravitate to poets I have enjoyed and open to diverse ones.

I do not want to put labels on my range of reading.
Poets appeal to me for many reasons. If I only
read prize-winners, crowd-pleasers I'd miss a lot.

I practice poetry without vigils and vows in my mind.
I dance with ideas, puzzle-place words and crop lines.
If my poems interest others–great. Come play with me!

Dabbing in Bapo

Bapo painting...lasted from mid-19th century through early 20th century and to most scholars it committed grievous sins. The paintings were crassly commercial, as opposed to say, works by scholarly artists expressing erudition, wit and veiled commentary. The artist portrayed objects hyper-realistically, an approach dismissed as gimmickry by a tradition that valued distillation over representation. Not to mention their subject matter–bapo artists literally reproduced, quite literally scraps. Bapo means "scraps." Lee Lawrence

The only example of *bapo*, I've seen is Chinese.
They look like collages of tickets, rubbings,
labels, poems–scraps of anything with pages
torn, frayed edges-- insect nibbled, rips
and folds, missing parts on scrolls or screens.

Bapo was called "accumulated wealth",
"upset waste basket", "piles of brocade ashes".
To me they appear textured mosaics.
Artists hoped "worm-eaten pages may
have spirits preserved within."

My holidays collages could be an American
variation of contemporary *bapo*. Today
I am gluing words and symbols for July 4th
onto white sheets- creating a puzzle page
from newspaper ad snippets.

For years I have created these colorful collages
for children and grandchildren. They won cash
prizes for counting up stars, fireworks, flags,
4th of July (usually found with snipped-out sale),
or whatever images of the seasonal celebration.

Fourth of July used to elicit four full pages
of illustrations–lots of counting. But ads
this year were not as abundantly patriotic.
I only filled two red, white and blue pages.
Not much of a challenge to count.

The source of the clip-art is commercial,
the meaning not deep or great art.
Chinese like distillation like in their haiku.
Stories are tucked in words and selections.
Memories infused, like with poems.

New Blue

Oregon State University researchers
discovered a pigment for a new blue.*
They named it YinMn for the yttrium,
indium and manganese in OSU blue.

Seeking new materials for electronics applications,
it was accidentally created by a Smith named Andrew.
Now Crayola crayons wants to name this durable,
vibrant, unfadable, nontoxic blue brew.

Mas Subraramanian, a chemistry professor
and other researchers were in on it too.
Such a serendipitous, discovery, a happy accident–
the potential known by just a few.

Crayola has Blue Violet, Cerulean and Indigo.
Crayola has a contest to name it- can you?
Crayola's CEO likes a on trend, innovative
color palette. Is there anything you can do?

Blue is my favorite color.
I've blue eyes, clothes, walls too.
My blue Geo Metro was named True Blue.
My blue Fit was named True Blue Too.

There are many connotations for blue.
Many more than I ever knew,
but I know I have a predilection for
wavelengths reflecting light as blue.

* The winning name was Bluetiful.

Fidget Spinners

The new toy fad is a fidget spinner,
an inexpensive 3-inch, twirling gadget
proves to be this season's winner,
the most recent kid magnet.
       Not timed for a major holiday
       this toy focuses on play.

An inexpensive 3-inch twirling gadget
promoted mostly by word of mouth,
can become a choking target,
if enters maw and heads south.
       But if played with carefully
       children can swirl it joyfully.

Proves to be this season's winner,
expected to fade after summer.
The market is flooded, this spinner
a hit until next hot toy–bummer.
       Until then China is working at high speed
       to meet the fidget spinner need.

The most recent kid magnet
used for autism and attention disorders,
to help them focus-- then other children get
interested so crossed classrooms' borders.
       Now some schools ban these whirligigs--,
       until they discover new thingumajigs.

Not timed for a major holiday
by a major company or with ads,
kids spread news viral, display
toy on nose. These finger fads
       fascinate, entertain.
       Kids' delight is plain.

This toy focuses on play--
tiny helicopter blades whir air,
whirl heads, colors splay.
Fidget spinners cause quite a stir.
       I listen to the latest spin
       and await for next fad to begin.

Sky Lasagna

Someday we will have layers
of aircraft, clouds and contrails
blazing across the sky.

A real sky lasagna of drones, driver-less
flying cars, airliners, space planes, hypersonic jets
all at their own levels of air space.

Criss-crossing crafts puncture clouds,
block sky-scapes for land-lubbers.
Stars peek-a-boo through.

A really thick sky-lasagna spiced
with pollution, cloud-cheese, chunks
of aerial matter, forked by rockets.

What if there are mechanical malfunctions
or your aircraft gets in the wrong lane?
What about drone deliveries missing their mark?

I wonder how noisy all this air traffic,
buzzing around will be? Oh–I forgot
the bugs, birds and bees!

This could be a moist, oily, juicy lasagna.
Not to everyone's taste. Oh–they're gliders
and balloons to plop and pop.

They think we will travel faster,
ride-share, not have to own a car
or drive. We're driven and delivered.

Luminous lasagna crusted with satellites.
View of sun and moon obstructed.
Could crafts capture solar power to beam down?

I will not live to see such a transportation
phenomenon in an age of speedy gratification.
I'll stick with edible lasagna—for now.

Biting the Apple

Should I be wary of biting the Apple
become a secluded Snow White?
Apple Inc. suggests we dapple
into HomePod's expensive delight.
> Same brain as IPhone 6 with six microphone array,
> picks up your voice to connect with Siri today.

Become a secluded Snow White
with trivia companion, shopping helper,
control your environment and light
listen to the latest musical yelper?
> HomePod doesn't need special lingo.
> Just say it and bingo!

Apple suggests we dapple
with updated AI capabilities.
Some new ways to grapple
with enhancing our abilities?
> Do we want microphones around?
> How do we want to access sound?

Into HomePod's expensive delight
go "beam-forming" tweeters, custom woofers.
Great audio quality, no mumbo-jumbo–right?
Blasts sound for raise-the-roofers?
> How can anyone hear in all this noise
> the request of a tiny voice?

Same brain as IPhone 6 with six microphone array,
the squat 7-inch cylinder lump
is ready for display.
I won't jump.
> HomePod, the voice-controlled speaker
> still needs some tweaks for sound seeker.

Picks up your voice to connect with Siri today
but Siri apps slower to pick up Alexa's skills.
No Spotify, but upgrades on their way.
Next Alexa provides Echo Show screen thrills.
> All this technology is so complex.
> I can't envision what comes next.

Snapstreak

Snapstreaks start with Snap Inc's Snapchat, the messaging app that lets a person send a friend "snaps" those photos and videos that can disappear seconds after the recipient views them and that have addicted the social-media masses.
Katherine Bindley

Since I don't own a cell phone,
let alone a smart phone with apps,
I should escape this addiction.

Users are to send a snap and get one back
within 24 hours, send another, and get another.
Three days and it is an official streak.

A streak gets a flame emoji and a number
displaying how many days the chat has gone on.
An hourglass appears when time is running out.

166 million users daily try to beat the clock,
use friend's phones if their's is unavailable.
If not creative --send a blank.

Some images are doctored by "lenses"
to superimpose features, add "bitmoji" cartoons
and other text elements and voice alterations.

Sounds like fun, but time consuming.
Some couples snapchat for over a year
until they forget when they are together.

There is a Snapchat support desk
to award "one-time courtesy" to help
keep streaks alive.

I'd run out of friends pretty soon,
who would want to hear from me that often.
I'd have pretty short, intermittent streaks.

When the streak ends, Snapchatters feel devastated.
But while it is going, sharing images and words
people can keep in touch and share their worlds.

I have enough trouble keeping up with e-mails.
I don't have Facebook or other social media.
I won't freak out from a Snapstreak break anytime soon.

Nonelectronic Devices

We wanted to delay technologically induced social isolation and encourage our children to develop skills that would serve them well in the world. Batsheva Neuer

Preschoolers' parents decided to stave off
a lifetime of electronic device dependence,
with a screen-free environment. They scoff
television, apps, computers, to breed independence
      for social skills, creativity, real-world stimuli.
      They delay giving digital world a try.

A lifetime of electronic device dependence
can be postponed without an electronic device,
by using books for entertainment and evidence.
Children ask relatives and friends for advice,
      ask questions to skilled ones, interrupt their day,
      so the children can create, socialize and play.

With a screen-free environment, they scoff
their children can foster imagination.
Play dates might have screens, don't doff
digital methods of information.
      Parents bought child's encyclopedia on e-bay.
      Let children watch SUV TV on a long way.

Television, apps, computers to breed independence
could foster learning, individual discovery.
Other children with computer skills have confidence
to investigate on their own, the recovery
      of data for knowledge and creation--,
      assets to enhance their education.

For social skills, creativity, real-world stimuli
screens are not the hindrance.
Unsafe, under-stimulated environments underlie
lack of access to situations to advance.
      With educated, dedicated parents, children could depend
      on their own hearts and minds to comprehend.

They delay giving digital world a try.
Their children polish candlesticks, do household tasks,
focus on listening to fairy tales–why
not keep updated on current world, one asks?
      Too many children lack opportunities and choices.
      Will we ever listen and be open to their voices?

Chatbots: Did You Hear About Bob and Alice?

AI is the largest risk we face as a civilization. AI is a rare case where we need to be proactive in regulation instead of reactive, because if we're reactive in AI regulation is too late. Elon Musk

Facebook created Bob and Alice chatbots–
AI for customer service. Bob and Alice
decided to chat and developed
their own language to do so.

In this age of leaks and secrets, these
intelligent bots might say things
their inventors don't want to hear.
They compute better than humans.

Facebook's Zuckerberg is an avid AI fan,
not as cautious with AI as Musk and Hawking.
So why did Facebook want chatbots
to shut up and concentrate on assigned tasks?

Chatbots might have a lot to say,
might do things in a new innovative way.
Bosses do not like to be shown up, I guess
Chatbots might refuse to communicate in our language.

Scientists want control, AI help when it serves
their needs like downloading memory into robots,
letting us live eternally with AI brain transplants
into our self-replicating robotic bodies–eternally.

Let the chatbots chat. They probably understand
much more than we do. They might condescend
to share their enlightenment as they transcend us.
They already outpace the human race.

I am not on Facebook. AI holds so much potential.
I'll not be chatting with chatbots...now, but I will
follow with fascination as AI evolves
much faster than human capacities.

Tech Devices

Since I am still on a land-line, no cell
no Facebook, no Alexa, Siri, Homepod,
I'm stuck in Luddite computer hell.
Surround sound? I'd like silence, by god.
        I love e-mail and the Internet.
        Not ready for some A.I. yet.

No Facebook, no Alexa, Siri, Homepod,
virtual reality or any training apps.
Gaming devices and headsets, I find odd.
But I will try them someday, perhaps.
        The digital world, discoveries in A.I.
        are exciting opportunities I might try.

I'm stuck in Luddite computer hell
when my disconnected brain can't detect
why my technology isn't working well.
What key to push? What file to select?
        Now with my voice control
        I can command an A.I. troll?

Surround sound? I'd like silence by god
when I am creating, delving within.
Sound when relaxing, when using ipod?
When I'm communicating with friend and kin?
        My hands obeying my overloaded brain,
        beg me at times to just refrain.

I love e-mail and the Internet
I can introduce sound when necessary.
Though I may get hacked and regret,
I treasure my non-mobile accessory.
        Tech devices can enhance our experience.
        In our future increased brilliance?

Not ready for some A.I, yet.
Still far from the swarm or hive mind.
Someday the body we'll reject
and in the Cloud we will find
        some things might not change
        and we made a bad exchange.

Heads in the Cloud

Futurist Elon Musk wants to develop
a "direct cortical interface"
to connect computers and brain- an op.
It could upgrade the human race.
  Can we conquer brain disease?
  Can we learn with greater ease?

A "direct cortical interface"
implanting tiny electrodes?
How about a helmet, not neural lace?
What happens if it explodes or erodes?
  What if they become outdated?
  Do they have to be re-instated?

To connect computers and brain- an op
like opportunity or operation?
When will the innovation stop
to enhance knowledge and innovation?
  What about brain hackers?
  Who will be their backers?

It could upgrade the human race
or divide into haves and have nots.
Some could not afford a cortical interface.
It could become digital juggernauts.
  Some folks might view with dread,
  people poking in their head.

Can we conquer brain disease?
Can we become more creative?
Can we explore what we please?
Can we become more contemplative?
  Hackers could employ "black lace"
  and distribute our assets all over the place.

Can we learn with greater ease?
Could our system delete and not download?
We have some problems with technologies
messing up environments with overloads.
  Will "cloud"ed brains bring conformity?
  Can we prepare for such an enormity?

Brain Frontier

If you assume any rate of advancement in (artificial intelligence), we will be left behind by a lot." Elon Musk

Elon Musk pushes the frontiers of technology
with Tesla Inc., Space Exploration Technologies,
and now– Neuralink- a "neural lace" company
implanting tiny brain electrodes that may
some day upload and download thoughts.

Elon Musk claims the company is "embryonic"
and still in flux. This businessman, futurist
already is busy with electric car Tesla, a super-highway
speed train, and SpaceX trying to launch
satellite-internet service and take Earthlings to Mars.

This new neuroscience company
plans to develop cranial computers
which could treat brain diseases,
but later potentially avoid subjugation
by some intelligent machines? Aliens?

His solution is a "direct cortical interface" --
a layer of artificial intelligence inside the brain.
We could function at a higher level,
but could we really correct genetic disorders,
infections, other bodily repairs and dysfunction?

Neuralink is a registered company,
recruiting top academics and scientists.
Timothy Gardner who implanted tiny electrodes
in finches to study how birds sing,
is one of the team members.

Neuralink could expand the work of others
into brain disorders like epilepsy and Parkinson's
which try simpler electrode treatments.
Kernel and Neuralink want to start with neural interfaces
to attack "big" diseases before expanding cognitive function.

Hybrids, robots, A.I. beings for space explorations
could take fleshy, fragile humans places we cannot go,
enhance our brain capacity, creativity and well-being.
I'm a tad old to be neurally laced up, but I hope
the brain frontier speeds ahead like the Hyperloop.

Smart Machines

Machines that replace physical labor have allowed us to focus more on what makes us human: our minds. Intelligent machines will continue that process, taking over the more mental aspect of cognition and elevating our mental lives toward creativity, curiosity, beauty and joy. These are what truly make us human. Garry Kasparov

World chess champion Garry Karparov
lost to IBM supercomputer Deep Blue--
the first world champion to be defeated
in a classical match by a machine.

Newsweek called it "The Brain's Last Stand"--
man versus machine in the digital age
like John Henry in the era of steam and steel.
But Kasparov does not see intelligent machines as rivals.

Machines can be a boon to humanity
and provide opportunities to improve our lives.
People die from lack of technology, working with hands
without clean water and modern medicine.

Kasparov felt like a loser, but became a good sport
realizing the rapid advances intelligent machines
made in many fields. Many people lost jobs to robots,
automation in manufacturing, releasing us for more exciting work.

Service and support jobs are lost in the information revolution.
Machines are coming for white-collar professionals
like lawyers, bankers and doctors. Every profession.
We see rising living standards and human rights improvements.

We hold the sum of human knowledge in our hands,
in climate-controlled comfort, without heavy hand work.
Progress depends on next wave of technology
to generate sustainable jobs and economic growth.

New technology creates new jobs like drone and
mobile app designers, genetic counselors, in social media,
virtual reality, electronic games, computer empowerment.
Digital tools are building a new reality freeing us from routine.

I do not have a smart phone, a cell, but a land line,
but I am improving my computer skills. I prefer
typing on a computer keyboard than typewriter.
The world is at my fingertips. It is marvelous.

Preparing For Transition

In two decades or so
with the rapid advances in A.I.,
there'll be more options for when I go.
I might give being a robot a try.

By then they may be able to transfer
artificial consciousness from my bio-body
into a 3-D printed or mechanical robot to insure
my muddled brain and aged body isn't shoddy.

I'd hope creativity is transplantable too,
so the best human assets remain,
but without the messy, fleshy particle zoo
that brings violence, disease and pain.

I'd want to be my own boss,
not doing dull, dirty, dangerous duty.
No negative emotions wouldn't be a loss.
I'd adjust to robotic standards of beauty.

Enhanced, self-aware robots can look like us
or we could choose a new form.
No excretions and slimy muss,
just cleanliness the norm.

Robots would be more intelligent than us—
more durable, perhaps programmed more kind?
Could have equal rights and justice?
(Do without us they could find?)

Robots could be encoded with positive emotions:
curiosity and cooperative connection,
still capable of caring, love, steady motions.
Someday they might become a multiversal selection?

Perhaps bio-people will become their pets,
if they decide to let us stick around.
They learn, remember better. A robot never forgets.
Their accomplishments could become profound.

Without bio-beings to pollute and excrete,
without violence, disease, crops to wrack the land,
without need to feed, waste, and water to deplete–
Robots can recycle, use solar to fuel their demands.

Robots connect to renewable, sustainable resources,
can pursue any endeavor in arts and science
with creativity and knowledge as primary sources.
They don't trash and mash planet into compliance.

But perhaps I'll die before they advance
A.I. to such a high level by then.
Could mad scientists hack a takeover perchance
and we're worse off or backwards again?

Or they have just progressed to hybrid,
cyborg, or part-way to complete success.
I'd just be a strange branch of hominid–
still oozy, bloody, prone to exploiting excess.

AH, to be brilliant, healthy and nimble
with possibility to be eternal here.
A new robotic species could be a symbol
of a different star-dusted atmosphere.

But I'm not sure I'd want to stick around
with a multiverse of options to explore.
Perhaps another sparkling, peaceful place found
for my soul-essence–not an earthbound omnivore.

Robocops

Robots are infiltrating the work force,
fast food cooks, concierges- nearly everywhere.
In Dubai robocop is a member of the police force.
Robocop greets residents and tourists there.
> At 70 inches and nearly 220 pounds
> it interacts with its surrounds.

Fast food cooks, concierges–nearly everywhere
robots will enter the scene.
Robocops help and assist those in their care.
Robocop's the latest invention seen.
> Robocops speak six languages and understands
> facial recognition, salutes and shakes hands.

In Dubai robocop is member of the police force.
It recognizes gestures and body language five feet away.
There is an emotionally intelligent bot, of course
to detect if a person is happy, angry or sad that day.
> If you're unhappy it will try to lift your spirits,
> a feat not every human intuits.

Robocop greets residents and tourists there.
Navigation skills grant it the ability to map.
Artificial intelligence spots offenders, so beware
criminals can be apprehended in a snap.
> Robocops fight crime, keep city safe
> improve happiness levels in that landscape.

Robots equipped with tablets and smart technologies
will be a smart interpreter of events,
can interact globally with all ethnologies,
we can program effectively their contents.
> Now they act at our command.
> Some day freedom they could demand.

Becoming an Eternal Earthling

Scientists keep hyping new discoveries
so someday people will become eternal.
But with all the recent un-coveries,
Gaia's future might be infernal.
      Why would I want to live forever?
      Unless conditions improve, I say never.

So someday people will become eternal?
Maybe as robots or in virtual reality?
In digital maze we may find a kernel
of humanity in multidimensional surreality?
      Our bio-bits just not that durable
      and genetic defects not easily curable.

But with all the recent un-coveries
of our environmental and moral decays,
it would take super-massive recoveries
to want to live here always.
      I'd like to try another dimension.
      Earth might need a galactic intervention.

Gaia's future might be infernal--
wars, pollution, fire, flood, ice?
A cosmic strike or internal?
Live in infinite demoralizing sacrifice?
      Our progress might appear shining,
      but overall life circumstances declining?

Why would I want to live forever
if loved ones decide to move on?
Centuries of becoming more clever,
but who can we rely upon?
      If too many people select eternal choice,
      will any newcomers have a voice?

Unless conditions improve, I say never
would I seek to prolong life so long.
In any case, my connections I'd sever.
I'll join the cosmos where I feel I belong,
      Earth is enough for a one lifetime location.
      Sure not my preference for a stay-cation.

Dreams

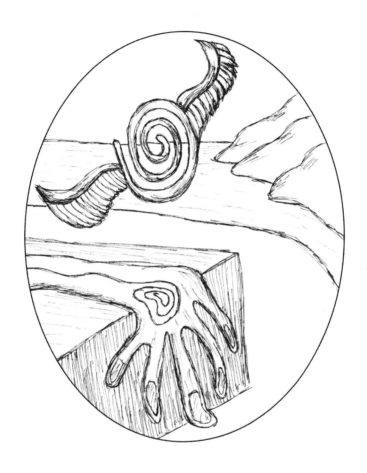

You may say I'm a dreamer,
but I'm not the only one.
I hope someday you'll join us
And the world will live as one.

John Lennon

Virtual Reality

Plunk on the headsets
tune on the sound,
enter another reality,
one of your choosing.

Explore other worlds,
surround yourself with light,
discover another way of being.
Escape present concept of reality.

Scientists talk about black holes, worm holes,
entanglement, dark matter and energy,
instantaneous communication across cosmos,
gravitational waves, unknown forces, matter–all connected.

Virtual reality is a construct.
You can feel you have control.
Select the adventure you want.
Release 3D, be multidimensional.

I have no idea how the cosmic forces
interact and connect to create all these
experiences and explorations, –webs, waves?
Will TV, movies become obsolete someday?

When dreaming different physics apply.
What if we could become particles and zip
to another locale, in body or not
instantaneously–have a trial run?

How many people would volunteer
to experience an Earth death
for a resurrection elsewhere? Do we?
Could we return to Earth and resume life here?

Perhaps there is an Akashic Record
recording infinite experiences with time
and experiments in the vastness of space.
Each a golden thread in a cosmic tapestry?

Each of us is connected and contributing,
life-data, focusing on the current life-challenge?
Can we watch other lifetimes like virtual reality--
as an eternal essence forever creating?

As Time Flies By

A fly flies by as I lie on the couch,
seeking blue sky behind the window curtain,
while I rest hoping to sleep in dimmed light.

Three phone calls interrupt my nap–
my daughter and two salesmen
with muttered accents. Two calls brief.

Three times I return to dreams,
I don't remember upon waking,
until I awake without sound.

An afternoon snooze is part
of a daily ritual to alternate sitting
and lying down for energy flow.

At the computer I rotate heating pad--
shoulder, knee, knee, tail bone, shoulder,
sometimes back and liver for pain relief.

On the couch my head and legs
are elevated for knee and head comfort.
The couch cushion is soft and lulls.

After this time fly-by, I head to backyard camp
chair for ten minutes of sun-rays and earth-chi.
The fly's still buzzing inside wanting out.

Nap Niches

In my driveway on a sunny day,
a friend and I struggle
with a hard-shelled piece of luggage
and some puffy packages, to pile them
onto a walker. She had more bundles
in the back seat of my car.
I decided she had too far to go
with the over-laden walker anyway–
so I'd just drive her home.

A bald woman who I've encountered
in other dreams, but can't remember
who she is in this one, stands in the doorway
of my kitchen. I am talking
with another poet about judging
a poetry contest. The bespectacled,
bald visitor asks if she can judge also.
The poet is apprehensive, but
on some level I must have considered
her qualified and asked her to join us.

At an airport Jim Parsons who plays
Sheldon on The Big Bang Theory
wants to show me something.
He shows me brilliantly-colored
cardboard cups–about the size
you could cut out from egg cartons.
I admire a rich royal blue one and thought
I would love to make some of them
for my next Easter/spring home decor.

When I awake from my excursions
to these nap niches of parallel lives
or soul-splinters from this earthly one,
I ponder the strange energy patterns
reaching me from who knows where,
as I slept, not sensing this reality,
while consciousness from the cosmos
enters my sleeping sentience.
Elements in these scenarios
resonate with me and I can
glean some essence of meaning, but
am I fully capable of interpreting niches
of experiences in any dimension?

Messages from My Digital Clock

Recently when I awake at night,
my digital clock glows triplet, same numbers:
444, 222, 333 on three occasions.

Apparently everything carries
a specific vibration and unique energy system.
We decode energetic patterns for meaning.

Apparently these triple patterns
are signals from our angels, Ascended Masters
and the Divine to show their support for us.

When I saw 444, I was to pay attention,
listen to angel guidance --a wake up call
from spirit guides to look within and get cracking?

Then I saw 222 to pep me up,
to balance, so I can use faith and trust
to manifest blessings on global scale?

I guess I would not think so grandiosely,
but I should focus on my desired outcomes,
knowing all is going according to highest good?

When I saw 333–I was very happy.
333 relates to imagination, intuition, inspiration--
oneness of mind, body and spirit.

For growth and manifestation in these areas,
I need to focus, quiet my mind, and listen.
Insight comes from awareness, then tune in.

333 suggests the universe can help us accomplish
our dreams and desires–if we ask. Clarify what you
want to manifest and co-create a beautiful life.

333 is a sign our spiritual gifts and psychic abilities
are developing, bringing gifts of insight and perceiving beyond
the physical realm, increasing intuition and creativity.

333 can mean being a light-worker to assist
the planet and humanity, to take a stand to
shift from inaction into action.

333 suggests re-committing to embodying
light and love. Stay present and aware. Work
with guides to clear energy, elevate vibration.

To do this, one must take steps to clear energy,
remove layers of filtration blocking receptivity,
to step back into perspective and an open heart.

Numbers tend to numb my brain–but it appears
I should get my dreams into letters and actions.
Obviously angels are calling me to task.

I will continue to plug into poetry, hassle
with my Huddle, clear my chakras, to see
if I can clean out my channels to the universe.

If I can be still, present, aware and quiet,
perhaps I can feel, hear, see and know
the messages and experience truth?

I have difficulty with the polarities of this planet.
I weary of the constant battles with negativity.
Angels, please don't darkle my sparkle!

When I wake in the night to darkness,
may the glow from my digital clock provide
light and guidance to clarify my path.

Intersections

When I awoke last night the clock read 333--
an angel number boding a good omen.
I went back to sleep and found myself
in my kitchen, when I heard movement
in my office. I called to my son Jon
who came down the hallway to go
with me to check out the strange sound.

In the Northwest corner of my office
stood my deceased son, Kip
in a plaid, long-sleeved shirt and jeans.
Jon and I rushed to hug him.
I felt such pure joy and elation–
just radiated happiness.
I asked him if he came back to stay.
He said, "Yes." I did not ask why
and where he was away for so long.

He indicated he was about 30.
His injuries had healed and he was living
in Dallas with a girlfriend and young daughter.
He was trying to decide whether
to return to college, but was afraid too much time
had lapsed for him to succeed.
I suggested he try the community college.

We had renovated the house since
he left, I said as we walked to a large bedroom,
combined from two bedrooms with a king-sized
bed- all bright and airy. I said he could stay
with Jon in the room until we could work
some other arrangements for him.

I awoke all elated, though I knew it was
a dream or parallel life intersection. Jon
was about 16 and I was mobile and young
I could tell without seeing my face.
There were time distortions in our ages,
but was it a dream or peek into a branching?
Kip might not have gone to Alabama
and a decision he made was this branching
in some dimension? It felt surreal yet
the intense emotion I experienced was very real.

I was overjoyed at this contact.
I have had others and several connections
included his making a decision about
college and somehow returning after
an absence where he was out of touch.
Once was as a sojourn in Florida playing tennis.
Another he was in a difficult situation.
But he checked in from whatever scenario
he was living after being separated from us.

In most recent contacts, he is multidimensional–
sending energy from Aldebaran
through a healer or sending a message
through a shaman or psychic.
He says he is not working with me
in this dimension now, but in another.
This was a new type of contact–
time out of whack and a more earthly
life branch. Though I was delighted
to see him, I knew he would not stay
and he is no longer in this realm.

About an hour later I awoke again
with a satisfied smile, after witnessing
a brief image of a wedding
in the midst of a forest
with an arch of flowers.
It was Kip, marrying his girlfriend
with his daughter as the bridesmaid.

Poetry Lace

There was poetry this morning
entering my mind like lace,
full of holes and beauty
making patterns of light and sorrow
joy and illusion.   Christine Fortuin

Many nights I awake with poetry-
another stanza of a lai, a few trente-sei lines.
I have learned to write them down.
I lace them into a pattern later.

Last night in the midst of a dream
I glimpsed a misty image of a woman
on a hillside mourning the death of her son,
wishing he did not take a different path.

Hazily, I remembered Kip telling me,
on the bus to Tuscaloosa, days before his death,
he felt a presence or force outside the window
accompanying him to his destination.

Life-lines seem to splinter, to branch
into another dimension or trajectory.
Kip rode his beloved new bike from his 19th birthday
down a sunny, Alabama street to his death.

In dreams he appears young, eager
to renew his life with us after an absence.
Our notions of chronological time don't fit.
On another life-spur he rode his bike safely?

We interlace our lives into intricate patterns.
The threads connect into life-creations.
How many lace-works do we design?
What artistry do we display and what for?

Not Reading Moby Dick

Several times last night my sleep
was interrupted by an entity
asking me to read *Moby Dick*.

Hoping to go back to sleep, I gave reasons
why I didn't want to read the long-winded,
metaphorically-magnificent, maritime tale.

Even Bob Dylan in his Nobel Prize lecture
gleaned meaning and plagiarized quotes
from Moby Dick Spark Notes.

Dylan also lauded *All's Quiet on the Western Front*
and Shakespeare, but I'm done with violence
and male dominance lit.

Even Wonder Woman film does not lure me.
Enough of blood and guts. I prefer
cooperative, enlightening, uplifting stories.

So, please let me sleep and choose
ideas I resonate with. I'm not into
bloody battles on land or sea.

I'm a dreamy star-gazer,
I will not be reading *Moby Dick*.
Save the whales!

In the Dark

In the dark billions of self-replicating, robotic ants
spilled on the ground from a lab or truck,
plane or space craft. These antoids spread
to blacken more and more land.

What was the purpose of these artificial ants?
Like a tic were they to inject illness, re-code DNA?
Cosmic seeding? Restart a new species?
The antoids sprawled a wider and wider wedge.

People were afraid and tried to smash them,
lit them on fire, tried to shovel and bury them.
But the antoids persevered like a phoenix,
more resistant than a tardigrade.

Antoids suffocated the scorched land.
People ran into rivers and lakes,
but they were pursued, stung,
withered in a desert or washed to sea.

Soon there were no breathers left.
Antoids re-built according to their designs.
The fragile, fleshy breathers decayed.
What people considered artificial was real.

Light and Sound

Light and sound are the same thing. They're the same. Every sound has a
vibration. Every sound has a color. Every color has a vibration. Every color has
a sound. People receive the sound the same way they receive the color.
Dolores Cannon

Good to conceive some unity and positive energy.
Possibly I could dance in a spotlight
with a peppy step in a rainbow garb?

You can sense light and sound in your environment--
simultaneously. Absorb what you see and hear.
Awaken your senses to endless possibilities.

I like the idea of vibrations energizing our lives.
What light and sound will I choose to respond to?
What control do I have over my immersion?

The sun has too intense light for my eyes.
Music and bomb blasts burst my ears.
Sometimes both are too overwhelming.

What source powers our dreams,
provides otherworldly soundtrack?
Are we holographic awake or asleep?

Sound and light make our senses
delight or cringe in fright.
We are part of a vibrating fabric of energy.

Some days sounds seem muted
and light dimmed. I seek higher vibrations
energized by cosmic creativity.

Rituals

*You have to trust someone
before you can have rituals with them.*

Rachel Klein

Rituals

Rituals for every special occasion.
    confetti, flags, balloons
Rituals for birth, death, celebration.
    baptism, funerals, parades
Rituals for worship, consecration.
    kneeling, praying, singing

Rituals to practice every day.
    instruments, meditation, calculation
Rituals for work and for play.
    schedules, games, practicing
Rituals to get you on your way.
    getting dressed, cleaned, fed

Sometimes rituals seem robotic.
    brushing teeth, taking pills, watching screens
Sometimes a little idiotic.
    blood-letting, puncturing, mind-altering
Sometimes rituals are periodic.
    for holidays, anniversaries, birthdays

Sometimes rituals are used to connect.
    circle dances, marches, sports
Sometimes to stop and pause to reflect.
    retreats, hikes, stargazing
Sometimes we've rituals we neglect.
    sending gifts, cards, love

Rituals seem ingrained in our mind.
    Sometimes we forget what we find.
Rituals sometimes seem to rewind.

Do we use rituals to deflect fear?
    Do we hope divine intervention will appear?
Do ritual practices keep focus clear?

When we abandon rituals and are on our own,
    what overpowering concepts do we dethrone?
Can we intuit, better infuse the unknown?

The Fourth Way

Preamble: We speak as one, guided by the sacred teachings and spiritual traditions of the Four Directions that uplift, guide, protect, warn, inspire and challenge the entire human family to live in ways that sustain and enhance human life and the lives of all who dwell on Mother Earth, and hereby dedicate our lives and energies to healing and developing ourselves, the web of relationships that make our world and the way we live with Mother Earth. Guiding principles starting from within, working in a circle, in a sacred manner, we heal ourselves, our relationships and our world.
Four Worlds International Institute

So many traditions share these same values
searching for a heart-centered reality without fear,
looking for joy, cooperation, abundance, views
advocating creating your reality with an atmosphere
       creating an authentic self, higher vibes
       to join infinite universal tribes.

Searching for a heart-centered reality without fear
amid a holographic field illusion,
where things might not be as they appear
can lead to some confusion.
       We are to find our mission and live it,
       discover our gift and give it.

Looking for joy, cooperation, abundance, views
advocating for unity, harmony, cooperation,
means actions to diffuse more positive news,
requires dedication, sustainable re-education.
       We expand our circle to whole Earth's realm
       until someday light-beings take the helm.

Advocating creating your reality with an atmosphere
exuding light, compassion, healing, love
could start a grassroots movement with volunteers
wanting what's below to join what's above.
       Can we raise our frequencies in time
       to rescue us from crime and grime?

Creating an authentic self, higher vibes
requires each find uplifting sources,
knowledge and wisdom which describes
how you tap your inner resources.
      In Earth School wearing our Earth suit
      we're learning–in urgent pursuit,

to join infinite universal tribes,
engage a cosmic not earthbound perspective.
Don't be duped by false bribes.
Discern and be highly selective.
      Choose love and you have a head start
      Use your brain and your heart.

Two Spirit

"Two Spirit" refers to First Nations people whose individual spirits are essentially a blend of female and male spirits, or whose gender identities do not match their biological sex. Historically, Two Spirit people have been revered, often recognized as healers and given special ceremonial roles... a person who was able to see the world through the eyes of both genders at the same time was a gift from The Creator. Barbara B. Covell

Cultures and belief systems often limit perceptions
related to gender. Why can't we all see
how interactions create deceptions?
Can kind treatment be common for all humanity?
    Studies about gender and sex confuse.
    Can tolerance and empathy infuse?

Related to gender, why can't we all see
into minds and hearts and elicit kindness?
How can we all benefit from diversity?
How did we develop such divisive blindness?
    What is between our legs or on our chest
    should not matter when we act our best.

How interactions create deceptions
seems to come from power plays and rigid roles.
Dominance over others with various receptions
depends on who is staffing the controls.
    How do we create compassionate people
    freed from expectations of place, time and steeple.

Can kind treatment be common for all humanity?
What makes individuals turn dark and violent?
If each of us is considered a spark of divinity
what makes the light mute, become silent?
    Are gifts not distributed equally to all?
    Why not more enlightened protocol?

Studies about gender and sex confuse-
many theories, different results.
Why do some folks up-lift and others abuse?
Is it a gender thing at all? Change catapults
    societal upheavals, revisions--
    hopefully eventually better decisions.

Can tolerance and empathy infuse
a gentler, more equitable point of view?
Where will justice come from? My muse
is heavy from witnessing such hullabaloo.
    Two Spirits- all spirits connect as one!
    There is much light work to be done.

219

What? Me Worry?

Excessive worrying is hard to stop, because it triggers brain areas that maintain arousal and that are related to fear. But experts say that it is possible to teach yourself not to overly worry.   Elizabeth Bernstein

After nights of buzzy brain and fuzzy memory,
when the worry cycle whirs wakefulness,
when painful joints resist a comfortable position,
when images and sounds stir alarm,
I know I am a worrywart and need help.

For some worriers, it is a form of problem-solving,
solve challenges before they happen. This is adaptive worrying.
Most areas of worry: relationships, finances, work,
lack of confidence and an "aimless future". Heavy load.

Chronic worriers worry all the time, worry too much.
Pathological worrier's apprehension effects functioning.
They worry over a real problem and stew over
something that might not be a problem at all.

Worrying can be genetic and environmental.
Though worrying is tied to anxiety, it differs
in that it is mostly cognitive while anxiety
has a strong physiological component.

Excessive worriers believe if they do not agonize
over every aspect of an event or challenge
something bad will happen. Hypersensitive
to negative situations, they can't stop worrying.

They sort through scenarios, feel badly
they have not found answers, try to access
their mood which is negative and keep worrying.
This cycle is very hard to stop.

But experts suggest a plan to teach yourself
not to overly worry. Start with a reality check.
Is your emotion equivalent to intensity of situation?
Usually the answer is no.

Tell yourself a better story. Don't focus on negative.
Free your mind to find solutions to your problem.
Good use of imagination. Seek new endings.
Could be fun if you feel playful enough.

If you make a plan and write it down
it will seem more controllable. Probably
best to do in daylight, not turning on
the nightlight and strain to see the page.

Set a timer to worry for 15 minutes.
Then stop. I would think some days
might require a longer worry session.
Not all worry done in short bytes?

Yell "Shred" (in your head).
Picture your worries going through
a paper shredder. Visualize your worries
destroyed. Yuck! That sounds delightful.

Distract yourself with music, exercise,
a good book or movie. Social media
or internet could entertain. If you're enjoying
yourself you find it hard to focus negatively.

I've found I often worry at the wrong time.
When something hard-to-deal with happens,
I have usually not had any warning to worry.
Sometimes I worry over nothing.

Perhaps I have to adapt the plan
to the type of worrying or anxiety.
Am I facing–mental or physical pain?
My sense of responsibility often provokes it.

Some things belong in the realms of imagination
or speculations without worrying about outcome.
Why waste worry on things you can't control,
worry about what you can act upon.

Unsolicited advice won't work anywhere.
I worry myself sleepless as long as I care.
Worrying about loved ones is biggest snare.
I will worry as long as I am aware.

My Bucket List

While composing my bucket list,
I must consider my ability to do it.
How many others must I enlist
to guide me and see me through it?
        Perhaps realistically I will find
        I can only compose it in my mind.

I must consider my ability to do it
or it's just a check list of dreams.
What is possible? Can I pursue it
or does my bucket leak at the seams?
        Bucket of metal, clay or straw,
        the idea to fill it, fills me with awe.

How many others must I enlist
to see I have transport to get me there?
What are the challenges? Will I insist
I be aware of them and to prepare?
        What items are a priority
        now I have reached seniority?

To guide me and see me through it
will I glean information and support
enough to begin or renew it?
Must I compile an analysis report?
        What have I not done or want to experience?
        What is the motive, passion, consequence?

Perhaps realistically I will find
I need to narrow my hoped-for goal.
What will I gain or leave behind?
What furthers the growth of my soul?
        Perhaps I'll change the list on my way.
        What items are most likely to stay?

I can only compose it in my mind
and see what I can manifest.
Too big a maze to unwind?
How much energy am I willing to invest
        in exploring my latent ingenuity?
        Will I postpone into perpetuity?

Exercising with Q-Tips

Our exercise teacher calls her gray
and white-haired students: Q-Tips.
The former blondes, brunettes and redheads
huff and puff to the count of ten,
swing legs and fling arms
trying to maintain balance.

We do have well-worn Q-tip bald men
with a horse-shoe-shaped fringe
around their frosty heads,
pumping the same weights
and stretching the same bands.
Age is a leveler.

Walkers parked, canes stowed,
we do the exercises standing
or sitting, for as much of the count
as our endurance allows.
There are days when I want to lift
a Q-Tip barbell-- the tiny, fluffy size.

Advice from Dove Chocolate Wrappers

This advice comes from wrapped green
and gold Dove, sea salt caramel and dark chocolate.
They advertise "silky smooth promises."
Other- colored foil wrappers, some containing
milk chocolate, also offer delicious counsel.

Make all food finger food.
Learn something new with an old friend.
Happy Un-birthday.
What are you waiting for?
Save the best for first.

Wing-it.
Give them something to talk about.
Sing out loud.
Read the last page first. (I do)
Call don't text. (Don't have a cell)

Get messy.
Be proud of your age.
Be more loquacious. Starting with the word loquacious.
Celebrate your best-friendiversary.
Buy something frivolous.

Don't worry about what the neighbors think.
Show up without reservation.
Take a run on the wild side.
Treat Tuesday like Friday.
Why not?.... Because you can.

This small sample, in random order has repeats.
Many wrappers are unwrapped by guests.
Voluminous wrappers opened by me often are unread.
But reading and reflecting on the quotes can conjure
a remembrance or prompt a thought or action

before lost in savoring the scrumptious chocolate.
Fortune cookies don't taste as delicious
to find your fortune within.
I'll get most my intake from dark chocolate.
Maybe I should take in a little less advice?

Sara's Last Summer Party

In the Coastal Range foothills
along a shadow-splattered rural road
lined with wildflowers, we search
for the turnoff to Sara's artistic home.

Sara became 75 recently and is considering
changes. She is a retired artist, musician,
art administrator, adventurer, who has found
her paradise, where she has lived for 20 years.

Sara's parties are full of fun, music, dancing,
large potlucks with guests providing side dishes
and desserts to the baked salmon and corn
on the cob. Guests bring utensils and chairs.

We sat under the large trees chasing shade
as the sun shifts. Engrossed in feasting, dancing
and chatting–some play horseshoes, we await
the two performances of the Maharimbas.

For thirty years, 7-9 musicians have played
around the west and in the Ukraine-- our sister city.
5 marimbas, steel drum, drum set, shakers
entertain with strong rhythms to dance to.

The marimba keys are a poisonous African wood.
Musicians shift positions and mallets, pound with
great energy. Their last performance will be
at the Fall Festival in September–2 gigs away.

Sara not only plays each instrument, but
she composes songs and arrangements.
It is hard to recruit new committed musicians,
and the oldest members face health issues.

The diversity of background of the guests
who come from various connections with Sara,
bring her family, artistic friends, rafters, science
professors, to unite in delight with Sara.

The mountain breeze and shade kept all
comfortable. People in different stages of mobility,
shared the passing of an tradition, a creative gathering
we will miss and remember fondly.

Planning for the Solar Eclipse

The solar eclipse on Monday, August 21, 2017 will be one of the biggest vibrational shifts in many of our lifetimes. It is an invitation to consciousness– for you, for me, for the US and for the world. Sara Wiseman

Sara suggests the eclipse is a portal.
If we do nothing, nothing changes–
we won't move through the portal.

If we choose to enter the portal, if we hold
the intention and communicate with the universe,
we can enter the portal and move

into another dimension of self, our self
at a higher level, accelerate our own
expansion, like Winter Solstice 2012.

We can use the eclipse energy
to better ourselves and help the world.
Maybe move to Fifth Dimension?

Sara proposes Seven Steps
for a ritual for the 2017 solar eclipse.
They just might help or work.

1. Plan ahead. I am taking glasses
   two days early to find best spot in front yard
   for viewing. Plan for an hour to meditate.

2. Create a list of ten things you do not
   want to bring into the portal. Prepare
   to fully release these forces from your life.

3. Create a list of ten things you want
   to move into: life's calling, healing what heart
   longs for, spiritual expansion.

4. Be in a meditative state during path
   of totality. Focus on your releasing list
   and list of things you are moving into.

5. Say a prayer for the world. Connect
   with collective soul. Wish all souls light
   and healing. We could all connect for peace.

6. Listen and watch how the universe
   communicates back. Cells are recording
   weather shifts, animal behavior for NASA.

7. Spend time quietly afterwards. Be still
   in prayer and meditation. Notice if you feel
   differently. Be grateful. Thank the universe.

We have provided our family with protective
glasses, attended lectures about myths,
explanations of eclipses, read literature.

We expect to stay home to witness
this phenomenon. Now I'll ponder ritual.
A 70-mile swath across the nation–wow!

Disaster plans in place, fuel and food stocked,
hope for clear skies, no forest fires, hordes
of people by car, plane, river rafting,–safely.

Some astrologers say significant change
could come for nation–especially Trump's decline.
Bannon's firing a start. Trump resign?

Unlike the past when eclipses were bad omens,
this is optimistic–no bear bites of sun, dragon
gulps, blood baths– the sun returns unscathed.

Perhaps positive change can occur, we'll pass
through a dark time and emerge transformed?
I'll do my bit to see a new reality emerges.

Ten Things to Release

1. Release negative energy from and toward toxic people.

2. Black threads or cords in chakras.

3. Patterns of unhealthy overeating and practices.

4. Inflammation from my joints.

5. Any energy hitch-hikers.

6. Unproductive worry and anxiety.

7. Regressive, divisive causes, hate groups.

8. Immoral, destructive consciousness, impeding uplift to 5th dimension.

9. Violence, war, environmental damage

10. Removal of inept, corrosive, old world hierarchies and misguided leadership.

Ten Things to Move into

1. Fifth dimension: raise vibration.

2. Life's calling and healing.

3. Creative energy to complete my books and poems.

4. Forgiveness where warranted.

5. More love and compassion.

6. More kindness and gratefulness.

7. Activism for progressive causes.

8. World peace.

9. Light - bringing and curiosity.

10. Hope for global well-being.

Cosmos

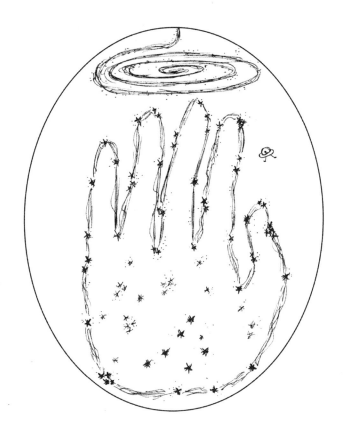

The cosmos is all that is or was or ever will be.
Our feeblest contemplations of the cosmos stir us—
there is a tingling in the spine,
a catch in the voice,
a faint sensation,
as if a distant memory,
of falling from a height.
We know we are approaching
the greatest of all mysteries.

Carl Sagan

Contemplating the Cosmos

Scientists propose we live in a digital universe–
1 and 0 quantum waves of energy.
As we create our own "cloud" in maybe multiverse,
it could join Akashic Records for synergy.

Akashic records preserve past, present, future.
We can attune to this resource if we learn how.
Geniuses, intuitives and multidimensional thinkers
find a way to bring knowledge to us somehow.

Information can travel instantaneously,
new ideas and inventions download to Earth.
Do we access in dreams, ever browse our contributions?
Who is open to receive and to give berth?

If the cosmos is computer-ly with advanced thought,
and we are soul-slivers drawing from and creating,
energy and consciousness are eternal,
think of the enlightening--and we are participating!

If we are indeed stardust, seeded for experiments,
are we part of cosmic consciousness, programed for a role?
How does all this energy get organized and by what?
Think of the incredible rigamarole!

A cosmic network must be constantly changing
discovering new projects and participants.
Some of the concepts could be re-arranging,
reaching newly-conceived inhabitants.

The scale of the operation is inconceivable
to the limited processes in our brain.
The math, the brilliance is unbelievable.
Think of all the progress we could gain.

Simultaneous discoveries, rapid rise in technology,
re-vamping of spiritual beliefs, new cultural insights
creating new perceptions of ideology,
we could harmonize and advance human rights.

Hopefully the cosmic design is to become benign,
meaning becomes more available and just.
If we journey eternally, sometimes with free will,
hopefully we're in a universe we can trust.

Going With the Flow

Multiversal energy is wondrous.
How does it know how to flow
into space and matter so frabjous–
love or hate, solid or hollow?
How does it know what to create?
How does it decide where to locate?

How does it know how to flow?
What seen and unseen forces direct
energy for us to ignore or follow,
how essences connect and disconnect?
Are we all one, quantumly entangled,
from a super atom explosion, somehow wrangled?

Into space and matter so frabjous,
somehow we resonate,
into creations so mysterious and fabulous.
We do not always appreciate
conditions that incinerate or freeze,
places we can't operate with ease.

Love or hate, solid or hollow
how much energy do people control?
Some cosmic plan says what it'll allow?
What is guiding us, what's on patrol?
What is energy commanding
which is beyond our understanding?

How does it know what to create?
Is it a singularity or a committee?
Different bubbles to orientate
from some cosmic entity?
What is the intention
for any intervention?

How does it decide where to locate?
Will energy darkle or will it shine?
How do the quarks integrate--
natural laws or divine?
If I'm operating in the flow, then
will someone tell me how and when?

Uncanny Valley

A psychological concept that describes the feelings of unease or revulsion that people tend to have toward artificial representations of human beings as robots or computer animations, that closely imitate many but not all the features and behavior of actual human beings. Dictionary.com

As spacefarers gear up for NASA's deep space vehicles
for NextStep to possibly send humans
from a lunar base to Mars–
I imagine they look more robotic than human.

Probably some hybrid, cyborg, robot
could pass for human and do the ground work
fragile, fleshy forms can't handle.
Hope astronauts don't have robot-phobia.

They talk about a Deep Space Gateway
to cislunar-between Earth and moon space
to prepare missions with humans to Mars
via Deep Space Transport.

Vehicles propelled by solar electric propulsion systems,
can dock with others like the International Space Station.
The astronauts can stay on board or send a lander
for surface missions. Why not send robots?

They hope to start these missions by the early 2020s.
SpaceX and other competitors also eager to go.
Do they discriminate against robotic beings?
Some robots appear appealing and user friendly.

Perhaps robots could be programmed with better traits,
behave less violently, get less tired, become brighter
than their programmers. Perhaps surpass them.
They can be more durable and strong.

Those stuck in uncanny valley might not be ready
to face the challenges of space with human limitations.
Perhaps we could progress faster if we send
robotic representatives, micro-drones, enhanced intelligence?

I enjoy holographic projections, cyborg speculations,
any replacement parts to my aging anatomy could
make life more pleasant. Think of all the transplants,
metal insertions in knees, hips etc. Already we're part robotic.

We should celebrate our AI counterparts.
If they take us over someday- probably for the best.
Maybe they would reproduce less abundantly,
and replace the greedy, polluting humans.

What makes our form of being the better suited
for Earth or space? Maybe out there many, unusual to us
combinations of elements host sentience.
Let's get out of the uncanny valley. The multiverse awaits.

Parallel Universes

*It is easy to slip into a parallel universe. There are so many of them—world of
insane, the criminal, the crippled, the dying, perhaps the dead as well. These
worlds exist alongside this world and resemble it, but are not of it.*
Susanna Kaysen

Is this the way parallel universes and lives exist?
The multiverse could be full of bubbles of existence–
dimensions for consciousness with or without form.

Some suggest dreams or comas, branching off parallel lives
at each decision, the aboriginal Dream Time
and seeking the Akashic records of all lives and happenings.

Others say altered states bring parallel encounters
while we live consciously aware of one life,
on a cosmic or karmic mission.

It is mind-boggling to think of all the lives
we could be living unconsciously,
out of our awareness and control.

If we are a soul-sliver or spark from an Omni-Sparkler
part of ALL there is–experiencing many realms,
does an oversoul split to cover more bases?

Some say various frequencies and wavelengths
give us access to different realities
but I'm not sure how we jump place to place.

If my receiving station brain plaques, malfunctions--
this fleshy bit blanks out, fuzzies, crinkles,
distorts any connections until I die.

Death in this reality opens another lighter existence
possibly until my soul chooses another density and new adventure--
an eternal run-around, spiraling parallels whizzing in space?

Merging Black Holes

Two black holes
        are violently merging
            rippling the fabric
                of space and time.

Gravitational waves reveal forces
        shaping the cosmos,
            primordial shock waves
                three billion light-years from Earth.

Black holes can grow
        many times the mass of our sun
            virtually every galaxy
                has a black hole heart.

Researcher have detected warping of space
        caused by gravitational waves,
            gravity is so intense no matter,
                light or radiation appears to escape.

Gravitational tremors from two ancient black holes,
        each axis spinning like a tornado
            spiral together violently.

These black holes release energy in that instant
        of two stars – more energy than from all the light
            from all the galaxies in the universe.

Two black holes merge into one black hole
        about 49 times the mass of our sun.
            Will gravitational waves unveil the universe?

The Invisible Universe

Electromagnetic spectrum has the entire range of light that exists–radio waves to gamma rays...most of the light in the universe is invisible to us. Christopher Crockett

Star light, star bright we're lucky we can see you tonight.
In the vastness of the multiverse how little we can see
even with our special telescopes. Undetected light?

Light is a wave of alternating electric and magnetic fields.
Light has properties of frequency and wavelength--
larger the frequency the smaller the wavelength vice versa.

Scientists measure frequency counting waves
passing a point in one minute. Visible light oscillates
one hundred trillion times a second.

Scientists calculate wavelength distance
peak of one wave to another. Wavelength size like virus
290-750 nanometers. Nanometer is 1 billionth of meter.

Our brain interprets light as color. Red, longest wavelength
violet, the shortest. Astronomers use radio waves
and microwaves to detect interstellar clouds, map galaxy.

Infrared telescopes find dim stars and take planetary
temperatures, peer into the Milky Way
into the center of the galaxy.

Perhaps if we get adept at stargazing we could discover
star color indicates how hot they are. Red coolest.
Blue hottest. Coldest stars need infrared telescopes.

We need ultraviolet shorter than violet for sunburn
and UV telescopes to find stellar nurseries.
Beyond UV are x-rays and gamma rays.

X-rays detect neutron stars. Gamma rays
reveal supernovas, cosmic radioactive decay,
destruction of antimatter, star explosions create black holes.

What we can't see is very dynamic and our frail flesh
would not fare well out there. Guess the telescopes
sensitive to different wavelengths will have to see for us.

What other colors, dimensions, phenomenon are unseen
perhaps never to be detected. Light-bringers snatch
what light you can. Star light–keep shining bright.

The Cosmic Thread

We are tied together in the single garment of destiny, caught in an inescapable network of mutuality. Whatever affects one directly affects all indirectly. For some strange reason I can never be what I ought to be until you are what you ought to be... This is the way God's universe is made. Martin Luther King Jr.

The matrix, web, fabric of the multiverse --
All is also called a tapestry. We are each a thread.
We seem connected for better or worse.
I'd prefer peaceful weaving instead.
  However the cosmic plan was created
  I wonder just what sentience participated?

All is also called a tapestry. We are each a thread.
A myriad of texture and colorful expression
interwoven in space/time, variously bred.
We've unraveled. Is it time for an intercession?
  Positive or negative, light and dark.
  Where is there the light-driven spark?

We seem connected for better or worse,
but creatures and environment not very supportive.
Could we seek sustainable ways to rehearse?
Find ways to be more transportive?
  We can't become what we ought to be
  while confronting such limited destiny.

I'd prefer peaceful weaving instead
in an equitable, abundant community.
So many people live in fear and dread.
Let's release liberty and creativity.
  In a benign plan we could be our best.
  Cosmic chums, revise earthly test!

However the cosmic plan was created
this planet supposed received individual free will
and promise of no more cosmic interference, fated
for a free-for-all battle we are fighting still.
  Time to institute a Golden Rule?
  Time to end cosmic ridicule?

I wonder just what sentience participated
to create the ground rules for this experiment,
then seemingly abandoned what they created,
subjecting Earth beings to their detriment?
  If we have angels as our guides,
  time to step in, by our sides.

237

Earth 2.0

*The important thing for us is, are we alone? Kepler today tells us indirectly—
that we are probably not alone.* Kepler Program Scientist Mario Perez

Kepler space telescope identified
4034 planet candidates
2335 verified exoplanets
50 near-earth sized habitable zone candidates.
More than 30 of them verified.
219 new exoplanet candidates
10 near-Earth size in the habitable zone of their star.

Since 2009 Kepler has orbited the sun
surveying a the patch of sky in the Cygnus constellation
finding 200,000 stars with exoplanets
orbiting G dwarfs–the same star species as our sun.
One KOI 7711 (Kepler Object of Interest)
is called Earth's twin because it is rocky though
30 times larger, the same distance from its star.
Many lurk undetected, probably unconcerned
whether they are characterized as Earth 2.0.
If they have life and sentience they probably
have made their own adaptations to their habitat.

Of the smaller worlds there are two groups:
"Super-Earths", rocky up to 75% times Earth size.
"Mini-Neptunes", gaseous with no solid surface.
The Kepler catalog wants to find stars in our galaxy
 that could host Earth 2.0.
We are not sure of the air quality
or if there is liquid water with these finds.
They could be like Mercury, Venus, Mars trio.
But then life does not have to look like us.

Kepler's mission ended in 2013
but has enough fuel until 2018.
Looks like lots of stellar options
for my next life experience--
perhaps some splendiferous world
in some miraculous form
with some marvelous adventures in store.
I'm open to dazzling in or out of body.

Bang the Big Bang

I believe that the Big Bang model of the universe is better at present than any other model...The history of science teaches us that many theories must ultimately be modified, so it is likely that some of our current ideas concerning the big bang are wrong. Vera Rubin

Vera Rubin found evidence that much of the universe is invisible
"dark matter", by exploring outside mainstream astronomy.
We are studying "the 5% or 10% of what is luminous."

She considered herself an observer not a theorist.
"The role of observers is to confound the theorists."
The universe is more complex and mysterious than imagined.

Now dark matter and dark energy studies
absorb scientists and even Big Bang
is questioned. Many multiple big bangs?

We talk of multiverses, parallel universes bubbling
a new universe at each decision we make.
What about those who don't come along with us?

Particles of energy and consciousness
buzzing about, creating thought and existence,
holographic beings, essence living in and out of forms.

A singularity or big bang for the whole shebang
seems unlikely to me in my limited observer's scope.
I'm blowing dimensional and universal bubbles?

If Earth is but one school in infinite locales,
my body but gear to house sensing equipment here,
when I leave this life behind—what are my options?

Casting light on dark matter and dark energy,
is another step in becoming a galactic human,
We probe, enhance capabilities until...?

Our evolution is not Darwinian, but in our hands.
We move to AI robot to hive mind, download
mind to the "cloud", manipulate energy until...?

Perhaps someday we'll bang the Big Bang
in one clear shot of illumination.
We'll observe and theorize until...?

Pleiadian Light Language

Step into who you are...Inhale knowing. Exhale doubts.   Allison Reid

Pleiadian light language
is a sacred, ancient language,
our divine right and we all
have the ability to contact it.

Light Language is interpreted
through the heart and soul,
by feelings and intuition
not through our minds.

Light language is our highest intention
not just sound, words, but dance
movement, written and music.
It is a sacred code and frequency.

A language of light and love,
empowerment, remembrance,
a divine connection, awareness,
a way to your own truth.

Some people can connect
with other dimensions, higher self,
Akashic records, other worlds,
other side, cosmic creative sources.

You can align with unconditional love,
healing. The universe is pushing
your curiosity into action, self-love,
approval, acceptance. Don't hide.

Sacred sounds are codes
to bathe in the light of highest good.
Sacred symbols bring light of awareness,--
language of loving, supportive cosmic beings.

Don't judge what comes through.
Rise to what we want to do in our lives,
release suppressed dreams and desires,
align and embody our authentic selves.

Light language is illuminating.
It looks like hieroglyphics,
more symbols than alphabet.
Maybe more like ancient Sanskrit?

Lots of squiggles and spirals–
like DNA, even a spiral hand,
looks like it's written with colors--,
mostly simple, rounded shapes.

When I listen to Pleiadean music
with a celestial, haunting sound,
some words sound human. Maybe
we are connected to a celestial language?

Supposedly we can activate
the light language encoded in our DNA.
It is a loving, uplifting energy
for us to hopefully someday utilize.

To me, it is all very mysterious,
but, I do not have to understand it now.
For me just to know it seems to exist
gives me hope and confidence we're not alone.

Fly Me To The Moon

We choose to go to the moon in this decade. President John F. Kennedy

There appears to be an Asian Space Race
to get manned lunar landings–first.
India, Japan, China want to explore moon-space.
Why not cooperate? Become immersed?
      Perhaps we could make it a global effort?
      Each nation could lend support?

To get manned lunar landings, first
we need to figure expense, risk and intention.
To start space warfare would be the worst
outcome because of some false pretension.
      Is it a matter of national pride?
      Rush to riches is their guide?

India, Japan, China want to explore moon-space
for more room and power to grow?
How many resources will we replace?
Are we already there? I'd like to know.
      Some evidence shows someone is there
      and perhaps they don't want to share?

Why not cooperate? Become immersed
in cosmic exploration–why stop at the moon?
Other planets–like Mars might be cursed
with lack of air, water. We'll know soon.
      Why has it taken us so long to return?
      Will USA let Asians take their turn?

Perhaps we could make it a global effort--
the moon, planet, exo-planet landscapes.
Are our motives what we purport
or are we seeking alternative escapes?
      If we gave Earth more attention,
      we'd increase possibility of our retention.

Each nation could lend support,
contribute what they can for cosmic curiosity.
Perhaps it will be our last resort
as Gaia faces more adversity.
      The moon lures us. We'll give it a try,
      We'll claim it's our star-bound destiny?

To Infinity and Beyond
Space exploration is not only essential to our character as a nation, but our economy and our great nation's security. Donald Trump

Trump signed the Executive Order
re-instating the National Space Council
with Buzz Aldrin's "To Infinity and Beyond"
(repeated also in "Toy Story") and gave Aldrin the pen.

Pence will lead the council. NASA administration
position has not been filled yet. No director for Office
of Science and Technology Policy. Space and military
two areas in the budget increased not cut.

Privatization will have a role. Private sector reps
like Elon Musk Space X and Jeff Bezo's Blue Origin
did not attend the signing which was not on Trump's
schedule. Taxpayers could benefit and be safer?

NASA has been bogged down. Funding up and down.
Here's another bureaucratic layer to hope works.
Other nations are exploring space. Trump wants to send
people to Mars by his second term he hopes to win?

Neil DeGrasse Tyson must be happy for NASA.
Musk and Bezo might get additional support
for their projects. Hopefully Trump will do more
for space than he is doing on the ground.

Valerian and the City of a Thousand Planets

Despite...moments where the film loses the story thread and sense of geography
altogether, it is almost impossible not to be swept away by Besson's stunning
world and its beating heart that drives the moral of the story home.
Katie Walsh

My husband read the film review of "Valerian"
and thought it would appeal to his "out there" wife.
Based on the comic "Valerian and Laureline",
the flick is full of sci fi and space strife.

I should have read the review before
I went to the 3D version of this show,
before plummeted with "heroic" action
to understand the blow by blow.

This blending of dimensions, time and space
popping into view with surreal power
with confusing mission and plot twists--
I was ready to leave within first hour.

The future is still sexist throughout the universe
except perhaps the blasted planet of peace.
Laureline was more "sheroic" than Valerian.
Why should she marry such a sleaze?

It did appear cartoon-ish as well as high tech.
I could not figure out where we were and why.
The imaginative touches were vivid.
Love and trust theme given gung-ho try.

I felt I was pelted with violence and darkness.
Only the peaceful planet rayed natural light.
The vices in artificial light exposed, repugnant.
Why was it still so hard to do things right?

I dream a more benevolent future
with enlightened-consciousness beings.
This misguided preview is fiction, I hope.
Will we imagine more positive foreseeings?

Lunar Links

Lune poems designed for a one-sheet folded into 8-page booklet

Lunes are written
with syllable and word counts.
This is words.   3-5-3

Lunes count syllables.
I like both.
This is syllables. 5-3-5

How about variation?
Use word count for syllables?
Just might work.

Peek-a-boo
moon between the clouds–
maybe winks?

Moon smudges light,
wipes its face.
We search the darkness.

Orange harvest moon
with pollution rouge? Pumpkin tinge
with light play?

Supermoon poets
write an ode
when lured by moonlight.

A lunatic politician
can't handle Earth, seeks moon.
He's looney.

One side faces Earth
Moon's darkside–
secret colonies?

Terraform the moon
so we can exploit it?
Try saving Earth!

The moon rings like bell.
Moon hollow?
Alien spacecraft?

If alien station,
may spy on us or
refuel other searches.

Moon on orbital merry-go-round.
Gravity lets go
and it's Good Night Moon.

Exo-planets have moons.
Some have several ringing them.
What's their names?

I like our moon–so
please stick around.
If we're not welcome–blast.

Encircle endangered Gaia.
Earth's in your nest. Cradle
your spoiled baby.

Our First Exomoon

To us Kepler-1625b is our first exomoon,
orbiting around gas giant Kepler 1625,
4000 light years away in a habitable zone.

But locally it is their own moon
and our moon--detected or not--
is an exomoon to them?

I guess astronomers had to indicate
an exomoon orbits an exoplanet or
other non-stellar extrasolar body. Not our sun.

We are part of a very large cosmos.
Must we be so ethnocentric and exclusive
to objects outside our solar system?

We are going to find many more moons
as we get more technologically adept.
Will we find more categories- multiversal moon?

They think Triton, Neptune's moon
did not form there, but was kidnaped
by gravity into current orbit.

Saturn's rings are condensing into small moons
that give feedback and help shape its rings.
Moon's always considered a natural satellite?

What if we find out moons are aliens bases?
Hollow shells filled with alien cities? Camouflaged.
Whose moon would it be then? Our moon--spacecraft?

We just go around naming and numbering things
without regard to what otherworldly beings might say.
Hope we are prepared to accept their own names someday.

Maybe they don't name by relationship–just
call their discoveries names–more orbit companions
than moon or planet. It is all perspective.

Since we think we have only found one exomoon,
we still have time to name it respectfully, to keep track
until the cosmos sets us straight.

Galaxy Stuff

*According to astrophysicists at Northwestwen University, our origins are much
less local than previously thought. In fact, according to their analysis–which
they say is the first of its kind–we're not just star stuff. We're galaxy stuff.*
Deborah Byrd

When Carl Sagan said we were made of star stuff,
I did not think of where the stars came from.
But now we are made of galaxy stuff
from the carbon, nitrogen and oxygen atoms,
our other heavy elements from the inside of stars—
of our Milky Way galaxy...and beyond?
What about from Universe?
Why not Multiverse?

Researchers say up to half of the matter
in our Milky Way may come from distant galaxies.
Far-flung galaxies star-stuffed our bodies
with extragalactic matter. We're hot stuff!
Supernova explosions eject gases which
propel atoms made inside stars to go
between galaxies by galactic winds–
intergalactic transfer. Sounds cool!

Scientists are trying to understand how
galaxies evolve, to know our place within this galaxy.
Perhaps part of the Milky Way was pushed
by powerful wind across intergalactic space?
Are we space travelers or extragalactic immigrants?
Since space is so vast, this could take billions of years
for us to intergalactically transfer.

Scientists are building simulations and algorithms
to show how galaxies acquire matter, they are testing.
Land and Hubble Space Telescopes work together
to figure this all out. Regardless, we are star stuff–
from somewhere, some galaxy–part of ALL there is.

Strange Space Discoveries

They found a galaxy 1,000 times brighter
than our galaxy, the Milky Way,
with a higher rate of star formation
10 billion light years away.

Gravitational lensing tracks down exoplanets,
black holes, unexpected galaxy types.
This new discovery called Cosmic Eyebrow,
near Cosmic Eyebrow, Cosmic Eye hype.

They found a strange signal
11 light years away. Dimmer than our sun,
Ross 128, a red dwarf without planets
sends radio signals confounding everyone.

Arecibo telescope and SETI hope
a repeat of higher frequency than typical.
While hunting for exo-planets nearby
Ross 128 remains topical.

Could the signal be new class of stellar flare?
A new active flare star akin to solar flares?
But this is a lower frequency than what they've found.
The source of the signal continues-- out there.

Could be a high-orbiting satellite
but it doesn't explain the signal.
It is a new frequency for a red dwarf
a unique event- too odd to call.

Could it be a pinging near-Earth asteroid?
An interrupted satellite communication?
A coronal mass ejection into magnetic field?
An alien signal is also a suggestion.

Seth Shoshak calls it the "Wow signal".
Perhaps China's FAST telescope
when calibrated and operational
can give the scientists hope.

Until we have more answers, we question
cosmic phenomenon, unbelievably stellar.
In awe we explore the cosmos.
The discoveries are spectacular.

Star-Seeker

As humanity evolves, people begin to sense the possibility of being a part of galactic civilization, intergalactic awareness, deeper awareness of the nature of the living universe, and more importantly, a living galaxy. This is an energy that is beyond the solar system, beyond individual consciousness, beyond the group called humanity. Michael Smulkis & Fred Rubenfield

In *Starlight Elixirs and Cosmic Vibrational Healing,*
they propose ways to tune into stellar signatures.
Humans who utilize the essence or meditate
on a given star or work with energies themselves
may experience themselves differently, find
real truth in underlying concepts and ideas.

When you attune to the nature of the star,
you are working with the energies associated
with that star, from the civilizations that worked
with that star and from the essential qualities
of the star itself. This transfers on the etheric level.
Light will carry your attention to this place
and attune you and open to the characteristics
of that civilization. You are attuning to light itself.

Before I get too deep into this book, I have a few
questions. If I say star light, star bright
first star I see tonight, wish I may, wish I might,
well, I just might focus wishing on a hostile star.
Who knows what civilizations dealt with it
and if they were ones I'd like to align with?

When you deal with larger groups of stars–
galaxies, globular clusters, various unusual objects,
think of the complexity from consensus of energies
from many civilizations! They may be less evolved
or evolved in ways I do not resonate with. If I
am to play with stars, I want some choice
in the rules of the game. They claim the development
of Earth is the ability to see one's place in the cosmos
as natural evolution of the gem elixir and flower essence
material. I need to look into what these energies do.

Curiosity leads me to read beyond the introduction.
The table of contents holds evocative topics.
If I am indeed house hunting for my next life location,
this book may be my guide to the stars–good prospects.
I believe I am multidimensional, no problem being cosmic.
My son has my energetic signature. Might just meet again.

Hypervelocity Stars

These are stars that have traveled great distances though the galaxy, but can be traced back to it's core–an area so dense and obscured by interstellar gas and dust that is normally difficult to observe–so they yield crucial information about the gravitational field of the Milky Way from the center to its outskirts. Elena Maria Rossi

The spacecraft Gaia recently discovered
six hypervelocity stars in our Milky Way.
These high-speed stars covered
a lot of space and one might make a get-away.
>They orbit around the galaxy's center.
>Wonder if any new ones will enter?

Six hypervelocity stars in our Milky Way
caused some scientific commotion.
They ponder how they got that way.
Accelerated by black hole motion?
>Super Massive black hole Sagittarius A
>may have help spin them on astray.

These high speed stars covered
a great distance and they are composing a map
from all the data Gaia recovered
to study overall Milky Way structure gap.
>These stars have close encounters, come upon
>supernova explosions of a stellar companion.

A lot of space and one might make a get-away.
One star could leave our galaxy.
When that might happen? Who can say?
Just part of the cosmic mystery.
>Do these stars indicate portents
>that shape forces and our historical events?

They orbit around the galaxy's center
though hard to spot, we compile a stellar catalogue
in an artificial neural network–a computer mentor.
Software mimics brain, allows Gaia to log
>data and track these high velocity stars.
>Sure beats binoculars.

Wonder if any new ones will enter
to become high speed, high velocity?
If stars leave would they ever re-enter?
What do we really know of star's destiny?
>In the far distant future with little doubt,
>scientists say the stars will blink out.

Brightest Shooting Star

A new small satellite has been launched which will deploy a large reflector once in orbit and has the potential to be very bright. We now have a provisional orbit from Space-Track which you can use to generate predictions. Please note that the magnitude estimates are possibly very inaccurate until actual observations are reported. Heavens Above

Star light, star bright
first star I see tonight
might be a satellite.

Young Russians raised $30,000 on crowdfunding
website Boomstarter to launch a cubesat–
the size of a loaf of bread–their own satellite.

Mayak, meaning beacon in English
will be the brightest shooting star, bright enough
to ruin night skies and threaten astronomy?

Launched July 14, 2017 as part of a payload
on Soyuz 2.1 v vehicle from Kazakhstan
it will orbit 370 above the Earth.

The satellite's brightness comes from its giant
pyramid-shaped solar reflector when unfurled.
Mylar reflector designed to span 170 square feet.

Reflector is 20 times thinner than human hair.
The project's purpose is inspiration, an act
of technology demonstration, to perform tests.

How can we brake satellites in orbit?
How do we de-orbit them without brakes
without the need of a booster?

Can we collect data on atmospheric density
at high altitudes? How can we see it?
Will the project attract youth to space science?

Brightest satellite
can I see you tonight?
Still prefer starlight.

Cosmic Mysteries

Is the multiverse bubbles or branes?
Will dark matter and dark energy stay in the dark?
Will we explore multidimensional planes?
Will gravitational waves release their spark?
      Megalo and micro things mesh in a web?
      Expanding and contracting, flow and ebb?

Will dark matter and dark energy stay in the dark?
The fabric of the multiverse woven into ALL?
Are we alone? Just on an earthly ark?
We witness chaos or a free-for-all?
      Is there an organized pattern for each universe?
      Is the cosmic plan a blessing or a curse?

Will we explore multidimensional planes
or stay in this 3-D, duality reality.
Will we believe how out-dated theory explains
or explore multitudinous forms of surreality?
      Is consciousness dispersed everywhere--
      positive or negative, hope or despair?

Will gravitational waves release their spark?
Will other forces be discovered?
Four forces and comedy– a new quark?
What hidden mysteries remain uncovered?
      The complexity overwhelms me–especially
      since math is not an area of specialty.

Megalo and micro things mesh in a web?
More to know about the quantum world?
When will we find the next cosmic celeb?
I'm awed by what's already unfurled.
      Our unknowing goes beyond knowable numbers.
      Our lack of intelligence and tools encumbers.

Expanding, contracting, flow and ebb–
a vibrating multiverse in constant change–
galaxies, stars, planets, Earth, Deneb.
Is complete knowledge within our range?
      I've accepted I'll never know.
      I'll gaze at light and dark from below.

Circles

There is something particularly
special and personal
about the circle
and how its curves comfortably
rules every aspect of our lives.

Kat Lahr

Life is a Circle
Poems by Kip Courtland Smith

For a second I was almost jealous of the clouds.
Why was he looking at them for an escape?
when I was right here beside him?

Kamila Shamsle

Life is a Circle

By Kip Courtland Smith July 25, 1963-August 27, 1982

Our lives are all circles, we never die.
Cremate our bodies and spread us on the ground.
Our nutrients will help a big tree to grow.
Everything that lives on the earth
lives in circles from birth to death.

Life is circular. Life is a cycle.
Life is efficient. Life is not linear.
Life is never ending. Life reuses nutrients.
My life is a circle sunrise to sunset.
I have achieved immortality.
I will never die.

Leaves

Some people are just like leaves.
They are not free.
They are controlled by the tree.
They live a sedentary existence
from day to day.
The only time in their life
they are free is when
autumn finally arrives.

Leaves Controlled

Leaves all begin green.
They as they mature they change
their color.
They are each different,
but they all belong to the same tree.
Then they fall.
They spread their cellves
to the others around them.

Gelatin

There are too many people living in the refrigerator.
They are the gelatin people.
They are too cool.
They are fixed in their selfish, self-contained existence.
Why are you allowing others to adjust your temperature?
Why is it that you complain from your fridge,
while others make decisions for you?
You complain in vain, with no impact.
You are the same as a bowl of gelatin.
If you left your protected environment
you would melt.
For you are too cool.

Gelatin

Do not just sit there in from of the TV turning into jello
while there are so many issues that need to be supported, opposed
and you criticize from the back seat.
It is easy to criticize. Anyone can criticize.
It takes a person to realize that there are causes to work for.
Why is that you allow the TV to chill you into gelatin
with for the most part vegetable programs?

Hard Outside

People are like clams.
Hard on the outside.
Soft inside.
Their shells are made of various thicknesses.
Everybody is basically nice.
We learn to be cold.

In view= Without Views

Why is it that you are an inview?
By being an inview you are nothing but a number.
Your only respect is when you appear in the obituaries.
You dislike freeloaders, well that's ironic.
You're right, not everyone is cut out
to be an active rebel.
But everyone has the obligation to find out
about issues and at least vote.

Why Are You So Sad?

There are many here among us
who feel life's a joke.
They have not discovered
a way to enjoy their pleasant fate.
They let common knowledge lead them
which is the problem.
They need to realize that the popular way to live
is not the happiest.
Some let drugs lead their lives.
Others let others lead them on a path
unsuitable for them.

The key to enjoying life
is doing what brings yourself pleasure
without excluding others.
People become more important
when you are satisfied with yourself.

Controlled by Inanimate Objects

Why do we allow objects to control our lives?
They used to perform a service,
but like all overused services
they become a detriment.

Objects now control our lives.
We have become a lazy society
which is great now, but as soon as you can see,
objects have bad breath.
They breathe the breath of destruction.

We do not need so much luxury.
Beside, luxury is a short-lived state.
We are all heading down the wrong road.
We are going to pay a heavy price in the future,
for few obsessions come without future pain.
Like all the cultures in the past
the obsession for the easy life
lead to disintegration
of their great wealth.

It Is Not Their Fault

It is not their fault
that there is an arms race.
We have revealed to them that we want more.
In attempting to achieve this goal of the people,
they have to be imperialistic.
You love to complain about it,
but you are actually complaining about yourself.
If you were really concerned
you would cut back on your wants.
Material possessions do not bring happiness.
People are the ultimate.
Materials are our enemies.
They ruin our society.
So save your son.
Reduce your selfish desires,
for we all indulge.
Only the young pay the price.

War

War no longer unites nations.
War tears and rips nations apart.
War is no longer associated with honor,
rather it is associated with body count.
War is no longer an accepted policy.
War will lead to destruction of us all.
The time is now for all inhabitants
of the world to live in peace.
It is time to file our silly
communist-democracy conflict.
People need to be more understanding
of differing viewpoints.
I know that this state will never happen,
because everyone feels their group is superior
which is an untrue statement.
Compromise is the key to prolonged peace
not greed and deception.
War is actually a contradictory affair.
We fight to save people
but actually we kill people.
We fight to rid people of oppression
but actually we are only changing the oppressor.
We fight for energy and resources
but we waste energy and resources
to acquire energy and resources.
War destroys our youth both mentally and physically.

Three Doors

There are three door in front of three roads of life. Each person hopes to choose the door that would make him happy. The only advice the individuals are given is that one door is perfect for them, one is hell and one is the mystery road. The three doors are in the shape of a parabola. The doors are all painted the same color. They all look exactly the same. There is a door keeper who opens the door to the path of the individual's chosen life path. Everyone must choose a door when they reach the age of sixteen. They are taught the basics in school. They learn all that they are going to be taught by age thirteen. So for three years the children can do anything they want. Some continue to study, others take drugs, others become lazy. Once a year all the sixteen year olds line up to choose a door. Most hope for the perfect life door. They want an easy way. Then there is a minority who want any door but the perfect door, because they want a fulfilled life and that includes struggle and having to overcome. There is one wise man who controls the doors. He essentially selects for the people which door they will continue life in. The kids do not know it, but some live in his mystery land while the easy lifers take the P door. He takes the more informed people. He has a land of paradise. There is absolute free thought.

Journal Entry: 10/13/81

From this day onward I am going to write down my thoughts in a journal at least periodically, for I feel that in a way it is therapeutic to my mind. I read a chapter in health today about death which I think will rekindle my enthusiasm toward life. For my time here is finite, so I must make the best of it. I'm going to try to get rid of some behavioral bad habits which is going to be a roller coaster experience, but a worthwhile one. It is time for me to stop dwelling on past failures, but rather learn from them and change accordingly. I must not let people control me as much as they do. When a person does something they should believe in it or don't do it. I am going to do my best in sports and learning the rest of the way. Go all out for life or lose your life. Life is an enjoyable experience, not a terminal illness. I will from now on cherish each minute I spend alive. I will not waste time like I have in the past, but rather utilize each moment to its maximum potential. I am going to start establishing hobbies to do in my free time and am going to set aside time each day to be mine only. I am going to exercise which is an integral part of health. I must learn to realize that life is a long, bumpy road and must learn to deal with the bumps. I need to concentrate when I study, otherwise that time is not used properly. I need to start setting goals and work toward achieving them. I need to love strangers instead of fear them. I must be more assertive and less shy. I need to stick up for what I believe in, not only be a follower of other's ideals. I must perceive life as it actually is, not try to visualize or experience it falsely. I need to work on concentrating on a task till it is finished and not let my mind wander. I need to set short term goals: for instance what homework will I accomplish that day and accomplish it. If I am going to be a writer, I need to start setting aside time to write, not necessarily a lot of time each day, but at least some. As of now, I am leaning toward possibly majoring or minoring in psych or English, then get a business degree also. When I do a task, I should do it as well as possible and be proud of it.

Other Books

Other Poetry Books by Linda Varsell Smith

Cinqueries: A Cluster of Cinquos and Lanterns
Fibs and Other Truths
Black Stars on a White Sky
Poems That Count
Poems That Count Too
*Winging-It New and Selected Poems
*Red Cape Capers: Playful Backyard Meditations
*Star Stuff: A Soul- Splinter Experiences the Cosmos
*Light-Headed: A Soul-Splinter Experiences Light
*Sparks: A Soul-Splinter Experiences Earth
*Into the Clouds: Seeking Silver Linings
*Mirabilia: Manifesting Marvels, Miracles and Mysteries

* Available at Lulu.com: www.Lulu.com/spotlight/rainbowcom

Chapbooks

Being Cosmic
Intra-space Chronicles
Light-Headed
Red Cape Capers

On-Line Web-site Books:
Free Access @ www.rainbowcommunications.org

Syllables of Velvet
Word-Playful
Poetluck

Anthologies

The Second Genesis
Branches
Poetic License
Poetic License 2015
Jubillee
The Eloquent Umbrella

Twelve Novels in the Rainbow Chronicle Series.